HOWARD BRENTON
& DAVID HARE

Pravda

METHUEN DRAMA

A METHUEN MODERN PLAY

First published in Great Britain by Methuen London Ltd
as a Methuen Paperback original in 1985.
Reprinted 1985.
Revised and entirely re-set 1986.
Reprinted 1990 by Methuen Drama
an imprint of Reed International Books Ltd
Michelin House, 81 Fulham Road, London SW3 6RB
and Auckland, Melbourne, Singapore and Toronto
and in the United States of America
by Heinemann, a division of Reed Elsevier Inc,
361 Hanover St., Portsmouth, New Hampshire 03801 3959
Copyright © 1985, 1986 by Howard Brenton and David Hare

Reissued with a new cover design 1993
Reprinted 1994, 1995 (three times)

British Library Cataloguing in Publication Data

Brenton, Howard
    Pravda: a Fleet Street comedy.
    I. Title   II. Hare, David
    822'914   PR6052.R426

    ISBN 0-413-58480-1

Set in IBM 10pt Journal by 🅰 Tek-Art, Croydon, Surrey
Printed and bound in Great Britain
by Cox & Wyman Ltd, Reading, Berkshire

Pravda was first presented at the National Theatre on 2 May 1985, with the following cast:

LAMBERT LE ROUX	Anthony Hopkins
DONNA LE ROUX	Zoe Rutland
ANDREW MAY	Tim McInnery
SIR STAMFORD FOLEY	Ivor Roberts
MILES FOLEY	Ian Bartholomew
REBECCA FOLEY	Kate Buffery
HARRY MORRISON	Ron Pember
HAMISH McLENNAN	Fred Pearson
BILL SMILEY	Richard Hope
SUZIE FONTAINE	Miranda Foster
MOIRA PATTERSON	Patricia Franklin
MICHAEL QUINCE MP	Peter Blythe
EATON SYLVESTER	Bill Nighy
DENNIS PAYNE	Christopher Baines
ELLIOT FRUIT-NORTON	Basil Henson
BEN SILK	Olivier Pierre
THE BISHOP OF PUTNEY	Daniel Thorndike
CLIVEDEN WHICKER-BASKETT	Guy Williams
MIKE 'WHIPPER' WELLINGTON	Ian Bartholomew
WAITER	Norman Warwick
LARRY PUNT	Marx Jax
DOUG FANTOM	Ian Bartholomew
LEANDER SCROOP	Nigel le Vaillant
PRINCESS JILL	Harriet Thorpe
'BREAKER' BOND	Bill Moody
HANNON SPOT	Fred Pearson
IAN APE-WARDEN	Olivier Pierre
CARTOONIST	William Sleigh
COMPOSITOR	Ron Pember
BINGO WINNER	Ivor Roberts
BARMAID	Jenny Galloway
PHOTOGRAPHER	Desmond Adams
JOURNALISTS	Robert Ralph
	Paul Stewart
	Glenn Williams

NEWSVENDORS, REPORTERS, ATHLETES, etc. played by members of the company

Directed by David Hare
Settings by Hayden Griffin
Costumes by Lindy Hemming
Stage Manager Diana Boddington
Deputy Stage Manager Karen Stone/Angela Fairclough
Assistant Stage Manager Graham Mitchell

Lighting by Rory Dempster
Music by Nick Bicât

A second edition of *Pravda* was first presented at the National Theatre on 2 May 1986, with the following cast:

LAMBERT LE ROUX	Anthony Hopkins
DONNA LE ROUX	Virginia Greig
ANDREW MAY	Peter Chelsom
SIR STAMFORD FOLEY	Michael Beint
REBECCA FOLEY	Phoebe Nicholls
HARRY MORRISON	John Bardon
HAMISH McLENNAN	Fred Pearson
BILL SMILEY	Christopher Baines
MOIRA PATERSON	Harriet Thorpe
'Y.O.P.' WORKER	Virginia Greig
MICHAEL QUINCE MP	Peter Blythe
EATON SYLVESTER	Richard Hope
DENNIS PAYNE	Jasper Jacob
ELLIOT FRUIT-NORTON	Basil Henson
REPORTER IN THE CLUB	Paul Stewart
BEN SILK	Olivier Pierre
THE BISHOP OF PUTNEY	Daniel Thorndike
CLIVEDEN WHICKER-BASKETT	Jasper Jacob
'WHIPPER' WELLINGTON	Paul Stewart
WAITER	Norman Warwick
LARRY PUNT	Craig Crosbie
DOUG PHANTOM	Olivier Pierre
LEANDER SCROOP	Desmond Adams
PRINCESS JILL	Harriet Thorpe
'BREAKER' BOND	Bill Moody
WOMAN JOURNALIST	Judith Hepburn
HANNON SPOT	Fred Pearson
IAN APE-WARDEN	William Sleigh
CARTOONIST	William Sleigh
BERT (PICTURE EDITOR)	Bill Moody
COMPOSITOR	John Bardon
BINGO WINNER	Glenn Williams
JOURNALISTS	
NEWSVENDORS	
REPORTERS	The Company
PHOTOGRAPHERS	
ATHLETES etc.	

Directed by David Hare
Settings by Hayden Griffin
Costumes by Lindy Hemming
Stage Manager Diana Boddington
Deputy Stage Manager Karen Stone/Angela Fairclough
Assistant Stage Manager Matthew Lynch, Martin Newcombe

Lighting by Rory Dempster
Music by Nick Bicât

ACT ONE

Interval

ACT TWO

ACT ONE

Scene One

An English garden. A parasol above a table, on the table a glass of Pimms. REBECCA FOLEY stands alone.

REBECCA. Home. Back in England again. A strange, still life. Everything misty. The low green English countryside unchanged. In the village church always fresh flowers on the altar. On the village green late in the season, the wicket taking spin.

She smiles.

The last party of summer.

ANDREW MAY *wanders on.*

ANDREW. Oh I'm sorry.

REBECCA. No I was just . . . wanting some air.

ANDREW. I don't think we've met.

REBECCA. It's my first day back. I've been in California.

ANDREW. Oh.

There is a pause.

REBECCA. Did you come alone?

ANDREW. Yes. I've been eating all the gherkins. I can't find anyone in there. They're so old. And dull.

REBECCA. They are.

ANDREW. They're so dead. Our host seems to attract all the most boring people in the Midlands.

REBECCA. He's my father.

ANDREW. I see. (*He blushes.*) I'm sorry.

REBECCA. No. Don't apologise, I feel the same way.

There is a pause.

ANDREW. Oh I think . . . now I remember, we heard of you.

REBECCA. Oh really?

ANDREW. Why did you come back?

REBECCA. I wanted to be cold and wet again. I missed it. The drizzle, the arguments, the way English people whinge all the time, about everything. I'd had too much optimism. Too many dazzling salads. I needed some grit again.

ANDREW. Oh well yes. I think that we have.

He smiles.

REBECCA. Have you been?

ANDREW. What? Oh, no. I work for your father, so I'm kept pretty busy. Also I sort of fear I'd like it too much.

REBECCA. You fear seduction?

ANDREW. Always. And you?

They look at each other.

Shall we go back in?

REBECCA. Yes. By the way when you say work . . .

ANDREW. Yes?

REBECCA. Work? Meaning what? I mean, what I'm saying is . . . to be honest, my heart is slightly sinking.

There is a pause.

ANDREW. Yes. I'm a journalist.

REBECCA. Fuck.

Scene Two

NEWSVENDORS, *carrying newspapers, come on. They deliver headlines.*

FIRST NEWSVENDOR. HEADLESS MURDER CASE: WHOSE HEAD IS IT?

SECOND. SEX TUTOR SAYS 'SHE LOVED ME'.

THIRD. TWELVE GO-GO DANCERS FOUND IN CRATE AT HEATHROW: TWELVE EXCLUSIVES.

FIRST. ARAB LOVE NEST HORROR. TWENTY-TWO HELD.

SECOND. ROYAL HAIR-DO. CUT OUT AND KEEP.

THIRD. GAY BISHOP. MP's PROTEST.

Meanwhile a female film star is pursued across the stage by reporters.

REPORTERS. Cindy! Cindy! Look at me. What about his wife?

CINDY. No comment.

REPORTERS. Cindy, Cindy come on give us something — Cindy it's our living.

CINDY. I just have this to say. Mr Ramero and I just love the Caribbean. There is nothing between us. The President of Uraguay is just a fun person.

Two REPORTERS *come forward, each with a notebook and a telephone crooked between shoulder and neck.*

FIRST REPORTER. The accused — two C's — said that Jayne — that's a-y-n-e Jephcott — that's ph . . . double 't' — had invited him windsurfing and that afterwards they had sex — that's s-e-x if you're wondering . . .

SECOND. The murder weapon, an open and bloodstained baked bean can, was found embedded in the murder victim's neck. Stop para . . .

FIRST. . . . on the sand under the soggy — that's two 'g's sail — that's s-a-i-l. The defendant, that's twenty-seven year-old Alberto Santin. I am a born again Christian . . .

SECOND. No I haven't actually got an interview but if I *had* an interview it would go 'interviewed today at her Colchester home the accused's wife said "I walked into the kitchen and I noticed that he was in an unusual posture. When I investigated further a metal object . . ." '

Meanwhile ANDREW *comes forward and addresses us directly.*

ANDREW. I love it. The smell of hot type. The thunder of the foundry. The nightly rush for the first edition. Oh God I love it so. The romance. All my career. The world passing through a newsroom. Processed, bundled and delivered through your door.

The set is now fully established. It is the Editor's office in an old-fashioned provincial newspaper. At the back of the office on a window, back to front in gothic lettering, are the words 'Leicester Bystander'. Outside the wood-panelled, green wall-papered office a corridor is seen to lead away into the distance. Discovered on the set is the Editor, HARRY MORRISON, a large man in his late sixties. He stands, with his elbows resting on a filing cabinet. On the top of the filing cabinet there is an old sixties record player. Bellini's 'Norma' is heard — beautiful, then distorted through the old machine. HARRY is standing with his back to us, in reverie.

NEWSVENDORS. Bingo! Bingo! Bingo! Bingo! Dingo! Zingo! Dingo! Congo! Bongo!

ANDREW comes on carrying a big notepad. The last NEWSVENDOR leaves the stage.

NEWSVENDOR. HEADLESS MURDER CASE: HEAD FOUND ON M1.

ANDREW (*quietly*). Harry?

Nothing from HARRY.

Harry?

Then HARRY moves. He takes the needle off the record. As he turns we see there are tears in his eyes.

HARRY. Dreams.

ANDREW. Sorry?

HARRY. No dreams, no life. Come in my boy, young Andrew.

ANDREW. The leader. I've brought a few suggestions.

HARRY. Go.

ANDREW. 'At this time of massive national recession, it is only natural that our youth should turn to trivial activities, in order to escape the grey reality of their lives.'

He looks up.

HARRY. Carry on.

ANDREW. 'The *Bystander* feels . . .'

HARRY. The what?

ANDREW The *Bystander*.

HARRY. The what?

ANDREW. The paper . . . you edit. *The Leicester Bystander*. Of which you are Editor.

HARRY. We are not the *Bystander*. We never call ourselves the *Bystander*. It should not be necessary. God does not call himself God. We simply exist. We are 'we'. 'We' say this murderer must hang. 'We' say this by-pass must be built.

ANDREW. Yes, Harry.

HARRY. Learn.

ANDREW. I am.

HARRY. Hang on to the style. Everything can go, but never the style. (*He intones:*) 'Nuclear power is not in itself a good or a bad thing. It depends entirely on the uses to which it is put.' Classical *Bystander* waffle, Andrew.

ANDREW. But . . .

HARRY. 'On the one hand . . .' (*He makes a firm gesture.*) '. . . on the other.' (*He makes a weak gesture.*) The lost art of leader writing.

ANDREW. I've written these notes. Do you want to read them?

HARRY. The job of the Editor is to prevent the balls ups! To do that it is hardly necessary to read every word. (HARRY *sits down behind his desk. He smiles.*) You know we didn't come out for Hitler.

ANDREW. I do.

HARRY. Hitler worked out very well for the *Bystander*. Because we saw him coming. It enhanced our reputation. Not that it wasn't a pretty close thing. I caught this phrase 'Mr Hitler is refreshingly dynamic'. Thought oh dear, not very wise.

Changed it to 'unnecessarily dynamic'.

HAMISH McCLENNAN has come down the corridor. He is in his early fifties, dour, balding, downbeat with a sheaf of galleys in his hand. He enters the Editor's office.

Good evening, Hamish.

HAMISH. Andrew. Harry.

HARRY. Fancy going for a drink?

HAMISH sits down with the enormous sheets which he lays out on a table. He begins to mark them out.

ANDREW. I'm sorry Hamish, I borrowed your count sheet. I had an idea about layout.

HAMISH. I don't work from a count sheet.

ANDREW. Really?

HAMISH. It's all in here, I can move anything around. (*He taps his forehead.*) Look at this, this is what I have to put up with. Here we have a photograph of a wedding over a story about a car crash. This got down to the stone. A marriage is described as a pile-up between an articulated lorry and a Vauxhall Viva.

HARRY. It sounds not unlike my own.

HAMISH (*to* ANDREW). Have you got the leader?

ANDREW. Well I, oh yes, I made a few notes. Possible opinions. For Harry.

HAMISH. Notes?

There is a pause.

ANDREW. I'll finish it now.

HARRY. Andrew's subject is the licensing of discos. Discos are, Andrew concludes, neither a good thing nor a bad thing. It depends entirely on the use to which they are put.

A YOUNG WOMAN dressed in punk regalia enters. She takes a sheet. She is on the Youth Opportunities Scheme.

YOUNG WOMAN. It's got ink all over it. (*She goes off.*)

HAMISH. Women's page! God, how I hate women's journalism. It's just me, I'm no good at it.

HARRY. You seem unusually downbeat tonight, Hamish.

HAMISH. Oh really?

HARRY. Positively dour.

HAMISH (*to* ANDREW). I need another letter on the fluoride debate.

ANDREW. Am I for it or against it?

HAMISH. Whatever moves you. (*He stands.*) I don't have sport.

He goes out into the corridor passing BILL SMILEY — a cheerful gangling man in his twenties, with a mop of fair hair and a brown corduroy suit. He is carrying a large brown paper parcel, rectangular.

BILL. Oh Hamish . . .

HAMISH. I'm sport-less.

He goes. BILL comes into the office.

BILL. Excuse me, but Sir Stamford's given me this.

HARRY. Sir Stamford? Where?

BILL. It's a painting. He wants me to hang it in your office.

HARRY. Sir Stamford's in the building?

BILL. Down in the print room.

He puts the painting down. HARRY is suddenly alert and on his way.

HARRY. Oh my God, first spot-check of the year. Furrow your brows, put ink on your fingers, expressions of enlightened concern. Firm but fair. Ah Miss Foley. Your father is with us.

REBECCA. That's right.

HARRY. Is this the proprietor's spontaneous visit?

REBECCA. I think it must be, Harry.

HARRY. Come on, Bill my boy, stay by my side. Drag him away before he makes any unguarded remarks to the workers.

BILL. He says he's on some sort of tour of the building.

HARRY looks behind him as he goes.

HARRY. Just . . . take my place will you Andrew?

They go.

ANDREW. Hello.

REBECCA. My father was coming, so I thought I'd call by with
him.

ANDREW. I was going to ring you anyway, about next weekend.

REBECCA. Ring me now.

ANDREW. Even better. What are you doing at the weekend?

*They smile and are about to move together, but are
interrupted by a middle-aged woman who has appeared a little
distracted at the office door. She is MOIRA PATTERSON.*

MOIRA. Oh excuse me, er . . . oh I wonder could you tell me?
It's just this morning's newspaper. A story on page five . . . I've
got it here.

REBECCA, *walking away.*

REBECCA. Andrew?

MOIRA takes out a cutting.

ANDREW. Are you a member of the public?

MOIRA. My name is Moira Patterson, and on page five you'll see
I'm identified as the owner of a health food shop whose son
Mark Patterson has been convicted of selling cocaine.

ANDREW. I'm sorry to hear that.

MOIRA. But I have no son. For that reason I'm afraid you have
the wrong Patterson. Could you arrange a retraction? To undo
it? Since eight o'clock this morning I've had no customers . . .
and if you could just publish a retraction in tomorrow's
paper . . .

ANDREW. Who was the reporter on this story?

MOIRA. Well, I don't know. It doesn't say.

ANDREW. Well. I'm not the reporter who wrote this story.

MOIRA. Can you tell me his name?

ANDREW looks at her for a moment.

ANDREW. I honestly can't comment on the facts in this case.

MOIRA. It's a simple thing. It's a couple of lines. Please publish a correction.

ANDREW. Look I'll be frank . . . it isn't very easy. You will find on most newspapers a policy, you see. The *Bystander* . . . sorry, 'we' . . . don't publish corrections. Because we don't like them. I'll be honest. They don't look good on the page. If every time we got something wrong, we published a correction then a newspaper would just be a footnote to yesterday's newspaper and yesterday's a footnote to the day before's. In fact, going further, now thinking about it, as I see it, look . . . a newspaper isn't just a scrap of paper, it's something that people feel they have to trust. And if they can't trust it, why should they read it? A thing is true or it isn't. So by definition, what is printed must be true — otherwise why print it? And if we apologise and correct, how can the readers know what is true and what is not?

REBECCA. You mean it's a matter — finally — of journalistic ethics?

From down the corridor, HARRY *is heard approaching loudly.*

HARRY. Hang on everybody, here comes the old fool.

ANDREW. Absolutely.

HARRY *comes on with* BILL SMILEY.

HARRY. Anyone seen the old Christmas balloons? Get 'em out, blow 'em up, come on Andy. Clear all that rubbish away.

ANDREW. It's tomorrow's newspaper.

HARRY (*to* MOIRA). Hello, I don't think we've met.

MOIRA. I own a small health food shop . . .

She is unheeded for HARRY *has moved on in anticipation of the arrival of* SIR STAMFORD FOLEY. SIR STAMFORD *is a man of distinguished appearance, in his late sixties.*

SIR STAMFORD. This way to the power house. The Editor's lair. Great issues of the day.

HARRY. Sir Stamford, do you know everybody? Our new Deputy Features Editor.

ANDREW. Andrew May.

SIR STAMFORD. Enchanté.

ANDREW. I was at your party.

SIR STANFORD. This is my daughter Rebecca.

ANDREW. We met.

REBECCA. In the garden.

BILL SMILEY *has got out a tray with a bottle of whisky and some tooth mugs on it.* HAMISH *has returned and now sits back down at his work without acknowledging anyone else.*

BILL. Here we are. Drinks for everyone.

HARRY. Miss Foley, will you take this in a tooth mug?

REBECCA. Thank you, Harry.

SIR STAMFORD. You don't drink Foley's, I see. (*To* MOIRA.) Who are you?

MOIRA. I run a small health food shop . . .

SIR STAMFORD *turns away.*

BILL. Look I'm just wondering, is the best thing that I take these sheets downstairs — put the paper to bed?

HARRY. No — no, let Sir Stamford look it over. No hurry.

SIR STAMFORD. Read the paper, good lord no!

An awkward pause.

Just give me the tip for the 3.30 at Sandown.

HAMISH. Arab Embalmer.

SIR STAMFORD. Hopeless. The usual *Bystander* donkey. No, it's my daughter feels strongly about journalism . . . Not an admirer of the *Bystander* I'm afraid.

REBECCA. I didn't say that.

SIR STAMFORD. Won't work with you chaps.

ANDREW. You didn't tell me that. You're a journalist?

REBECCA. Isn't everyone?

HARRY. Too true.

REBECCA. I wrote for a radical paper in California. Lifestyles, micro-chips, the body. Now I'm freelance — that means unemployed.

HAMISH. Sir Stamford . . .

SIR STAMFORD (*to* ANDREW). Do the honours my boy.

Harry, this is for the *Bystander.* A picture to hang on the wall.

BILL SMILEY *reveals it. It is of a race horse, standing in a green meadow. There is a silence.*

HARRY. A horse, Sir Stamford?

SIR STAMFORD. Yes. Southern Colonel. The greatest sire of one-and-half milers. Grazing in the picture, outside Louisville, Kentucky.

He smiles.

Of course you may always hire Southern Colonel. For one hundred thousand pounds you can get him to roger your mare. But I concluded the really smart thing would be to buy a share in him.

HARRY. I see.

SIR STAMFORD. That way you can get him to roger at will.

HARRY. Yes. I can see that makes sense.

REBECCA *frowns.*

REBECCA. Dad . . .

SIR STAMFORD. Oh it's infinitely better. If he knows he's going to have more than one go at it, there's far less chance of his breaking her legs.

HARRY. *Does* he know?

ANDREW (*to* HAMISH). What's he talking about?

There is a pause.

SIR STAMFORD. I have been offered a share — a one-eighth share — in Southern Colonel. The price is one and a half million pounds.

There is a silence. REBECCA *looks anxiously between them all.* HARRY *grave now.*

HARRY. I see. I see. Short-term capital is that what you need?

SIR STAMFORD. I am considering a sale of one of my assets.

HARRY. Ah yes.

SIR STAMFORD. I am not sure in the interests of the Foley stockholders it any longer makes sense for us to maintain our presence in communications.

HARRY. Communications, is that what we are?

There is a pause. BILL SMILEY *watching and waiting.*

SIR STAMFORD. Harry . . .

BILL. I do have this problem. Excuse me. I've got tomorrow's paper in my hand. I need the Editor's approval . . .

HARRY. It is withheld. I take it I am still the Editor . . .

SIR STAMFORD. Harry, old man, come come, you're speaking to a Foley . . .

HAMISH. Take the bloody thing.

HARRY. Hamish, I countermand your order. The captain will not surrender the wheel.

ANDREW. Rebecca . . .

REBECCA. I had no idea.

SIR STAMFORD. I am rationalising this paper . . .

BILL. You mean getting rid of it?

SIR STAMFORD. Harry, you may or may not remain as editor, according to the wishes of the incoming proprietor.

HARRY. Right! Who is he?

A pause.

HARRY. Are you going to tell me his name?

A pause.

Well I mean, I can guess. There aren't many people trying to buy newspapers these days. It's usually the same old three.

SIR STAMFORD. I promise you . . .

HARRY. The three lepers. Which one is it this time? Is it the bent lord who made his money in rubber goods?

SIR STAMFORD. Viscount Mangrove has not been a bidder.

HARRY. Then it must be that Nazi who sells cheap holidays to the Copacabana?

SIR STAMFORD. Sir Hector Prize is Rebecca's godfather. I would never sell this paper to a personal friend.

HARRY. So it's Gilbert Zenith. I don't mind working for crooks. I've worked for one, begging your pardon Sir Stamford, but with Zenith it's a physical thing. Have you ever been in a lift with him?

SIR STAMFORD. The bid has come from beyond these shores. That is as far as I'm willing to go.

REBECCA (*after a pause*). Dad, please tell us.

SIR STAMFORD. It's a very hard name to say. Apart from anything else, there is litigation. If I mention his name, there are repercussions. After I have said his name it is important there are no impromptu or spontaneous remarks. Any man . . . rising . . . seeking to do something . . . to achieve, in the world . . . is liable to attract, as we newspaper folk understand, enemies, hysteria, hatred. Put these thoughts from your mind. Approach this name in a positive context.

REBECCA. It's Lambert Le Roux.

There is a pause.

HARRY. Who?

REBECCA. That's who you were lunching with.

SIR STAMFORD. Yes, it is Lambert. I like him very much.

BILL. Le Roux?

HARRY. Who is he?

SIR STAMFORD. He is . . . a man . . . from the Southern part of Africa.

HARRY. You mean he's South African?

SIR STAMFORD. As I said. He is a South African. Of impeccable liberal credentials.

ANDREW. So he's black. That's interesting.

SIR STAMFORD. Not black.

ANDREW (*not bearing*). The first provincial English paper to be owned by a black man . . .

SIR STAMFORD. Not black. Though through no fault of his own.

REBECCA (*staring in disbelief*). This paper is sold to a white South African?

ANDREW. Oh, God, I know who he is.

BILL. The sportswear king.

ANDREW. He runs that cricket. I read a profile on him.

BILL SMILEY *suddenly interrupts, the sheets still in his hands.*

BILL. Look, I have to say, speaking personally, this is just a personal thing, I don't really want to work for a racist . . .

SIR STAMFORD. Now that is exactly the kind of impromptu remark I begged you all to forgo. I shot an elephant with Lambert Le Roux.

HARRY *goes up to* SIR STAMFORD.

HARRY. Right. Look me in the eyes, Sir Stamford.

He lurches down onto his knees.

Do it in person. In the old family way. The way it is done amongst gentlemen. More whisky! Put a glass in my hand! Don't your sort like to be there? Walk the rheumy old dog out into the yard and shoot him in person?

SIR STAMFORD. Harry . . .

His voice cracking with emotion.

This is not an emotional thing! This is a business decision. I need money. It is not here. It is out in the Kentucky blue grass.

BILL. Then why . . . I mean, why this Le Roux, why does he think otherwise? I mean, just the most basic thing, this paper makes a profit. Just a small one. But a profit all the same.

With sudden assertiveness.

It's as if you all *want* to give up, roll over and let it all . . . go to bits. I don't get it. It's as if that's what you want.

A brief pause. MOIRA *speaks quietly.*

MOIRA. I understand you all have this new proprietor? Does anyone know, is there a chance he might publish corrections?

HAMISH *suddenly gets up and goes and seizes the galleys himself.*

HAMISH. I'm going to take this damn thing down there myself.

HARRY. Hamish, you come back here.

HAMISH *turns and confronts him angrily.*

HAMISH. Don't fuck with me, Harry. I've taken ten years of your shit.

BILL. Hamish . . .

HAMISH. Is incompetence meant to be charming? Shambling and muttering and drinking, it's meant to be lovable, is that right? Opera, while other people work? Well, that joke has passed me right by.

HARRY. Have you betrayed me? Have you been doing deals?

REBECCA. Jesus, this is terrible.

HAMISH. Clear out your desk.

HARRY. You've talked to him, haven't you? This Le Roux?

To SIR STAMFORD, *pointing at* HAMISH.

Was this Judas there at your lunch?

Suddenly HARRY *runs at* HAMISH *and jumps on to his back. A stumbling struggle.* HARRY *is pulled away and held by* BILL *and* ANDREW.

SIR STAMFORD. Harry, this will do you no good at all.

ANDREW. Look, I must warn you. The staff won't wear this. Will we?

BILL. Certainly not. We'll strike.

ANDREW. That's right.

SIR STAMFORD. Oh God!

BILL. No it's possible. Your whole organisation. Pickets at the gates. NUJ blacking.

ANDREW. Secondary action.

SIR STAMFORD. Industrial relations in England! All this greed, all this bitterness . . . why can't we just agree among ourselves?

BILL. You can't buy and sell people. They do have rights in the matter.

HAMISH *flings down the galley sheets.*

HAMISH. I just can't believe the stupidity of this. You talk as if you had some power. Do you not even realise basics? Divest yourself of your fantasies. We have a new owner. The business is sold.

SIR STAMFORD. I wouldn't say that.

HAMISH. It was sold at two-thirty.

SIR STAMFORD. A process of consultation has begun. Talking to the staff in respect of their wishes. Canvassing opinion.

HAMISH. You signed the contract at lunch.

SIR STAMFORD. Well, it's true I certainly discussed a commitment.

REBECCA. Commitment?

SIR STAMFORD. Undertaking.

HAMISH. You went to the Midland to bank the fucking cheque.

SIR STAMFORD. Yes, well that is true.

He looks at HAMISH unblinking.

But I also felt . . . in honour . . . that a process of staff consultation should begin.

A pause. Everyone is appalled. There is a tear in SIR STAMFORD's eye.

We all hope to be forgiven if our actions . . . are misunderstood.

REBECCA. Dad, you've sold the paper for a horse. That's all. Some deal over steak and kidney pudding. Don't ask them to cry for you.

Pause.

HAMISH. I am now ready to begin my period of editorship. In practice, I've been the editor for eight years. Covering for this drunken clown . . .

HARRY. I resent that.

HAMISH. Now there comes a man — I must admit I found him surprisingly charming . . . his wife is Natal free-figure ice skating champion . . . and he's prepared to recognise my talents. Unlike you, Sir Stamford. You just let me carry the work, without acknowledgement. Now I say to you all: the locks have been changed.

Suddenly HARRY lurches across the office to his desk where he scrabbles in a drawer. He finds a razor-blade.

HARRY. Dignity. Where's my dignity?

He mounts the desk holding the razor-blade aloft.

BILL. Oh shit, Harry.

HARRY (*trying to roll up his sleeve*). This blade was given me by a survivor of the great Beaverbrook massacre of '52. And I vowed that if I ever found myself in this position . . .

HAMISH. Somebody grab him.

BILL. A heroic gesture.

ANDREW. Too much opera.

HARRY is trying to attack his wrist with the razor-blade. ANDREW and BILL attempt to restrain him.

BILL. Er, how do we do this?

HARRY. My blood is on your head, Foley.

SIR STAMFORD. This is humiliating. Rebecca, please leave the room.

BILL *suddenly reels back with blood dripping from his hand.*

BILL. Oh shit, God, help, I've cut my hand.

HARRY. Are you all right, Billy?

BILL *rushes across and grabs a galley to stem the blood.*
MOIRA *is already there, poring over the galleys, which she now takes to* HAMISH.

MOIRA. If you're the new editor, I can use this little space here. To save my shop. And my life.

The telephone on the desk rings. They all stop.

HAMISH. The editor's phone. I'll take it. Harry, get off the desk.

HARRY *crawls off the desk.* HAMISH *lifts up the telephone.* HARRY *moves on all fours across the room.*

Bystander. McClennan.

HAMISH *goes on listening down the telephone. Then he moves the receiver away from his ear.*

It's Lambert Le Roux. I'm too closely associated with the old regime.

He puts the receiver on the desk and crosses to the far side of the office.

He wants another new editor.

He suddenly shouts at the top of his voice.

What does he think I am? A fucking football manager?

REBECCA *walks across and picks up the receiver. Quietly.*

REBECCA. Hello.

There is a pause. Then she holds out the receiver.

Andrew it's you.

Scene Three

At once the stage clears. Then deepens. And heightens. On to the empty space walks LAMBERT LE ROUX. He is in his early forties, heavily built, muscular and dark haired. He is wearing a dark suit — plain, anonymous, of the greatest quality.

LE ROUX. You are born into a tragic culture. Tragedy is bred in your bones. A country of almost impossible beauty. From the very moment you are born, the sadness infects you. Like a mist hanging over the veldt.

Jackal, giraffe, hyena, lion — the well-nigh unimaginable richness of creation is presented to you every day from the window of your speeding car in scenes of almost post-card-like glamour. Nature is there. In front of you.

Childhood, boyhood, manhood. These are special things in South Africa. The hardening of muscle, the sprouting of hair. The coming realisation you are born into a divided culture. Ski-ing, riding, scuba-diving, flying your private plane, you feel all around you — and below you — the tragedy of the condition from which you cannot escape.

No one has tried harder than I through my organisations to untie the knots of the cultural contradictions — black, white — rich, poor — us, them — but people who come from Europe bearing simplistic solutions ignore the grandeur, the scale of what we have inherited from Mother Nature herself.

What I do is a natural thing. There is nothing unnatural about making money. When you are born where I was born, you do have a feeling for nature. What I admire about nature is — animals, birds, plants, they fucking get on with it and don't stand about complaining all the time.

Above the arena a huge banner unfurls with the legend: SPORTSWEAR INTERNATIONAL — WELCOME TO FRANKFURT. There is a motif of Olympic rings. We are in a huge featureless exhibition hall. An enormous open space, totally unfurnished. At ten-metre intervals, telephones are placed on the floor in lines. With multiple echo, a woman's voice makes a bland, incomprehensible announcement.

LAMBERT LE ROUX *moves across to greet* MICHAEL QUINCE MP. *He is in his late thirties, with a slightly vain air. He has thinning hair, is in a perfect suit, with rings on his white hands.*

QUINCE. My dear Lambert.

LE ROUX. Michael. Welcome. You found your hotel?

They shake hands.

QUINCE. Yes, thank you. I love the Holiday Inn. No surprises. And you're looking well.

LE ROUX. Fit.

QUINCE. It's so long since I was in Frankfurt. They hadn't built this place. I think it's now the greatest exhibition hall in Europe. Marvellous. The security men, those air-conditioning ducts.

LE ROUX. It's the right place.

QUINCE. It's so good to escape from the House of Commons. Everyone thinks MPs are always off on freebies. If only that were true. Personally, I enjoy them shamelessly. We work bloody hard. And most of what we do goes unremarked, unrewarded.

LE ROUX. Yes. It's a choice.

QUINCE. As you say.

There is a moment between them.

I do have to thank you for that marvellous article.

LE ROUX. Think nothing of it.

QUINCE. In *The Daily Tide.*

LE ROUX. It's a pleasure. 'Man of Steel'. (LE ROUX *smiles.*)

QUINCE. Very good picture. Slightly minimal prose. I do think of all the hard-hitting tabloids in Fleet Street yours is much the most deliciously down-market.

LE ROUX. That's the nice thing about having picked up one or two foreign newspapers. They are a way of doing some favours to my friends.

QUINCE. Yes . . . I'm sure.

LE ROUX. Though not everyone wants to be in the *Tide*. With all my dirty vicars and randy divorcees.

QUINCE. Well, I was very grateful.

LE ROUX. It's nothing. I'm a businessman, first and foremost.

QUINCE. And brilliantly successful. The diversity of your interests is sometimes bewildering.

LE ROUX. That's right.

QUINCE. Hotels, newspapers, international sportswear.

LE ROUX. Yes.

QUINCE. Anything that improves the quality of life.

LE ROUX. I'm sorry?

> EATON SYLVESTER *arrives. He is a tall man with broad shoulders. He is wearing a light suit. He is Australian.*

SYLVESTER. Ah, there you are.

LE ROUX. This is looking very good.

SYLVESTER. And I see you have the man.

LE ROUX (*to* QUINCE). This is Eaton Sylvester, my business manager. Have you met Michael Quince?

SYLVESTER. No, but we did you in the *Tide*.

QUINCE. That's right.

SYLVESTER. Good pic.

LE ROUX. 'Man of Steel'. Now we'll put him in our upmarket paper.

SYLVESTER. *The Leciester Bystander.*

> SYLVESTER *and* LE ROUX *laugh.*

QUINCE. I didn't know you had that. A provincial British paper?

SYLVESTER. Up 12.7.

LE ROUX. We've got a good man there.

SYLVESTER. Lambert's never met him.

They smile.

He doesn't need to meet him. He's doing nicely. The paper's O.K.

LE ROUX. Anyway I went to the English town called Leicester. I had a steak and kidney pudding. It was enough.

They let QUINCE *hang for a moment. So to fill in, he gestures round the area.*

QUINCE. Well you've certainly chosen the dominating position. Your sportswear stand is resplendent.

SYLVESTER. We're putting down a running track. Sandpit. We've taken over areas seventy-one and seventy-two. All of that is ours.

LE ROUX. The prime sites.

QUINCE. Tremendous.

SYLVESTER. We're here for six days.

LE ROUX. Eaton is expecting to have done all significant business before the Trade Fair opens tomorrow. Eaton is a genius at selling.

SYLVESTER. I like money passing through my hands.

LE ROUX. He knows both sides. He worked for the Australian Government.

SYLVESTER. I'm a naturally brilliant accountant. It's luck.

LE ROUX. When he was twenty-three he was number two on a Royal Commission.

SYLVESTER. Into building scams on civic contracts. Who insulated the roof of the Sydney Opera House with lavatory roll? Then I realised the people I was investigating were more interesting than the people I was working for. In Government service in Australia you get a lot of low calibre dickheads. Fuckwits, do you have those in England?

LE ROUX *smiles at* QUINCE. QUINCE *looks uncomfortable.*

LE ROUX. Please relax, Michael. You don't leave this place doing anything you don't want to. None of us will.

QUINCE. No, I know that.

LE ROUX. Good.

QUINCE. I'm here with a completely open brief from the British Olympic Committee. With a mind to the next Olympics in Seoul '88. To award the concession for sportswear to whichever of the many competing firms, including your own, which I judge best. Like all amateur sport we need money — and if the price is wearing some of this beautiful clothing . . .

LE ROUX. Yes, it's a tricky decision. Well, you must see the whole hall tomorrow. Make sure you've done the right thing.

QUINCE. But I . . .

DENNIS PAYNE *is approaching across the area. He is about thirty-five with classic blonde looks and a pitted face. He is wearing a scarlet shirt with the* LE ROUX *flash across it, pale pink trousers, mauve cricket pads with large yellow stars on them. He is carrying an aluminium bat and a futuristic green helmet.*

LE ROUX. Ah, Dennis, there you are.

QUINCE. Goodness me.

PAYNE. We heard a rumour you were here.

LE ROUX. You look splendid.

PAYNE. I've been ready for a while. I'm doing a centre spread for the *Tide*. Photo feature. On the future of English cricket.

LE ROUX. Do you know Michael Quince?

QUINCE. I recognise you from the Long Room.

LE ROUX. This is D.P.P. Payne.

QUINCE. My God it's Dennis Payne. Essex and England.

PAYNE. It's true. I am.

SYLVESTER. Dennis was actually Captain. During the great bouncer war.

LE ROUX. Dennis kept getting hit on the head.

PAYNE. That's right.

QUINCE. Well I think the umpires should have intervened.

LE ROUX. Oh no. Dennis should have stepped out of the way. (*He turns and speaks to* PAYNE *as if to a moron.*) How are you finding the new gear, Dennis?

PAYNE. It's a little too early to say. I'll need a good session in the nets. But my first impression is really quite favourable.

LE ROUX. Michael is here to do business for England.

PAYNE. Ah, good.

LE ROUX. If you need Dennis he works in the sales team.

PAYNE. Speciality, cricket.

QUINCE. All, well, that's interesting. Do you . . . ?

QUINCE *pauses.*

LE ROUX. What?

QUINCE. No, I wondered . . . as an ex-captain of England, his views on the size of the flash.

A silence. LE ROUX *lets him spin.* PAYNE *looks at the ground.*

LE ROUX. Go on.

QUINCE. Its vulgarity. With the Olympics we are dealing with national representation. The flash is ostentatiously large, quite overwhelming the red, white and blue. (*A brief pause.*) We would also like a new brand name, a name that was rather less . . .

LE ROUX. South African?

QUINCE. Oh good Lord, no. I mean yes.

LE ROUX *crosses the area and stops way away from them.*

SYLVESTER. He's rude.

QUINCE. For myself, I love cavaliers, the buccaneering spirit. I feel at home with people like you. But I also have to deal with current sensibilities. And the image of British athletes running around the track advertising South African sportswear . . . the idea of it needs to be . . . massaged. What

I'm saying is . . . (*A brief pause.*) Why not cut the flash down and call yourself Carruthers?

LE ROUX *looks at him beadily. Then with sudden ferocity.*

LE ROUX. Have you seen your British team? Running ragged-arsed, bare-bottomed round the track? All white elbows and knock knees? Wiping their snot on their vests? Looking like a chain gang escaping across the moor? Dropping with beri-beri? Is that what you want, Michael? To be associated with failure, disgraceful failure?

SYLVESTER. He's got a point.

QUINCE. Well they won't actually win, whatever they wear.

LE ROUX *looks at* QUINCE *for a moment.*

LE ROUX. There is only one criterion in life, Michael. To succeed.

SYLVESTER. Like God.

LE ROUX. So what makes you think I want to kit out your team in the first place?

QUINCE. But that's why I'm here. You invited me, you rang me up, you offered me a flight . . . a hotel . . .

SYLVESTER (*to* PAYNE). Get this, Dennis?

LE ROUX. The flight is yours. Have it. I will not reclaim it. Buy nothing and you may still fly back.

QUINCE. So I should hope.

LE ROUX. People say it is you who are the racialist but it is they who will not do business with me because of the country I come from.

SYLVESTER. Too right.

QUINCE. No really, please . . .

SYLVESTER *has unzipped a black leather briefcase.*

LE ROUX. Is this the portfolio of his mother's personal finances?

QUINCE. What?

SYLVESTER. Every penny the old dear's got.

LE ROUX. Eaton, please.

SYLVESTER. Too abrupt?

LE ROUX (*to* QUINCE). We have obtained this document from your mother's accountants, Hamstring and Dooley. (*A pause.*) We are greatly interested in your mother's holdings in the *Victory*.

QUINCE. *The Daily Victory*!?

LE ROUX. Acquiring it.

A long pause.

LE ROUX. Oh, I know what you will tell me. *The Daily Victory* is one small part of your country that you all say will never be for sale. An Everest of probity. Unscalable. The only newspaper with England on its masthead. An institution, like Buckingham Palace, the Tower of London, and your two Houses of Parliament. And as dismal and dreary a read as it is possible for humanity to contrive.

QUINCE. It's true, it isn't very good.

SYLVESTER. Your mother owns twenty-one per cent of the shares.

QUINCE. I don't understand. If you want to acquire stock go and talk to her.

LE ROUX *smiles at* SYLVESTER.

LE ROUX. It is often hard to speak clearly to Dame Elsa.

QUINCE. Ah.

LE ROUX. Your mother is a very remarkable woman. A great humanitarian. And ornithologist, as you know.

QUINCE. Yes.

LE ROUX. My wife has visited her park in Suffolk. With our two children. Seen your mother's very happy birds. But she is often inaccessible. Her mind is often drifting between one thing and another.

SYLVESTER. Incoherent. Senile.

There is a pause. QUINCE *is looking at them shrewdly.*

QUINCE. I gather from what you're saying you've already offered for her shares.

LE ROUX. Yes. Dame Elsa seems not to realise the potential of her shareholdings. Her mind is always on young ospreys — and their eggs.

There is a silence.

QUINCE. Oh God is there nowhere to sit down?

SYLVESTER. Dame Elsa's stock and we own 53 per cent of the shares.

LE ROUX. Control.

QUINCE. Yes, but you . . .

LE ROUX. What?

QUINCE. Can you just *buy* a piece of England? You're South African.

LE ROUX. We have the England cricket captain.

PAYNE. That's right.

PAYNE *beams happily.* LE ROUX *is smiling at him.*

QUINCE. Just like that? There are trustees. With a veto on ownership. Do you suppose they'd ever let you in?

LE ROUX. But what if they did? And you were the man who had helped me? Some backbench lobbying? The right word here and there? You've not much to lose. And if we succeed, a friendly *Victory* will assist your career.

QUINCE. I see.

LE ROUX. As a politician? Not even a politician, no longer a politician, with *The Daily Victory* behind you, a statesman.

A pause.

LE ROUX (*to* PAYNE). Get him a seat.

PAYNE *goes off.* QUINCE *has moved forward as if to think the issue out.*

QUINCE. The press and politicians. A delicate relationship. Too close, and danger ensues. Too far apart, and democracy itself cannot function. There must be an essential exchange of information. Creative leaks, a discreet lunch, interchange in the lobby, the art of the unattributable telephone call, late at night — 'A source close to the Prime Minister', meaning 'the Prime Minister'. Yes. This mutual relationship *is* a good thing, and if it can be made concrete, formalised by an actual commercial arrangement . . . If I, for instance, were to offer you my private skill and influence, and in return you were to guarantee me access to your newspapers, if the channels of free expression were to be . . . (*He pauses.*) . . . channelled in my direction, if 'Man Of Steel' were to be a regular feature, a column, written by myself, by me then democracy would be safeguarded. And we would have a very satisfactory deal.

There is a silence.

SYLVESTER. How soon can you speak to your mother?

QUINCE. How soon do you want me to speak to my mother?

LE ROUX. In the next thirty-six hours.

PAYNE *has returned with an extremely small stool of garish modern chrome design. It is nine inches high.* QUINCE *sits down, a little gnome,* LE ROUX *and* SYLVESTER *tall above him.*

QUINCE. Fine.

Scene Four

NEWSVENDORS *come on to the stage as* ELLIOT FRUIT-NORTON, *the Editor of the* Victory, *is pursued by* REPORTERS. *Meanwhile behind them the set for Scene Four is being assembled.*

FIRST NEWSVENDOR. MYSTERY BUYER AT 'THE VICTORY'!

SECOND. THORNTON-HEATH SEX-TRIANGLE: FOURTH MAN NAMED!

THIRD. 'VICTORY': THE CRISIS DEEPENS.

FIRST. CUT-PRICE HOLIDAY KING SAYS 'I'M NOT IN THE RACE'.

Meanwhile the REPORTERS *are chasing* ELLIOT FRUIT-NORTON *in the same manner they hounded the film star* CINDY. *This time there is also a TV crew with sun-guns.*

REPORTERS. } Mr Fruit-Norton. Look at me! Look at
PHOTOGRAPHERS. } me! Elliot! Elliot!

ELLIOT FRUIT-NORTON *stops to hold an impromptu news conference. He is a tall, stooping man in his mid-fifties, supercilious, with raddled boyish looks.*

FRUIT-NORTON. Ladies and gentlemen, please, we are members of the same profession.

There is quiet.

As Editor of the *Victory* I am being kept hourly in touch with all developments at this great national newspaper. I wish to assure our readers of the continued existence and high standards of this great national newspaper. Of which it is my privilege to be Editor. *'Nole vocem publicam tangere ne bonum patriae interrumperes'.* Thank you.

FIRST REPORTER. What?

SECOND. Fuck me.

THIRD. Does that mean you are still Editor of the *Victory*, Mr Fruit-Norton?

FRUIT-NORTON. My own position is not in any way at issue during the current negotiations. Clear the way, please.

He strides off. The REPORTERS *rush after him. The TV crew follows.*

REPORTERS. Elliot! Elliot! Mr Fruit-Norton!

While the NEWSVENDORS *take up new cries.*

FIRST NEWSVENDOR. EDITOR TO GO!

SECOND. EDITOR DENIES IT!

THIRD. BLOOD-LETTING AT 'THE VICTORY'!

FIRST. LATIN-SPEAKING EDITOR EATS HEARTY BREAKFAST!

The set has, meanwhile, been assembled. A gentlemen's club of the utmost distinction is suggested by twenty high leather armchairs. They face in many different directions, some all together turned away from us. We are in the Irving Club. ANDREW MAY *and* REBECCA FOLEY *are wandering in as the last* NEWSVENDOR *goes.*

SECOND. TOFF'S PAPER TEARS ITSELF APART!

There is a moment's pause as ANDREW *and* REBECCA *stroll among the chairs.*

REBECCA. My God.

ANDREW. This is it.

REBECCA. Is this what men do together? Men sit in high leather chairs.

ANDREW. We do. We are firm, we are confident, we are often fast asleep. I wonder how you get to be a member?

REBECCA. Oh you have to believe the right thing.

ANDREW. How do you know the right thing?

REBECCA. If you have to ask that you'll never belong.

Enter a WAITER. *He is very old, in a white coat, has white hair and shuffles.*

WAITER. Sir?

ANDREW. What?

WAITER. Drink, Sir?

ANDREW. I . . . er . . . oh . . . what . . . I . . . What do people have? A spritzer.

REBECCA. Two.

ANDREW. And a cheese sandwich.

WAITER. Two spritzers, Sir. Cheese sandwich.

ANDREW (*smiles*). Oscar Wilde's drink.

WAITER. A dead member.

ANDREW. Sorry?

WAITER. Mr Wilde was a member of this club. Ireland's greatest writer. 'Course, writing that well, they pretended he was English.

ANDREW. Yes.

WAITER. Then they put him in gaol.

The WAITER *turns and goes.*

ANDREW. Goodness me.

REBECCA. What a strange setting. He does choose oddly.

ANDREW. Rebecca, we promised to behave.

REBECCA. Well I will. I find the whole idea of meeting this man irresistible. I'm curious. I'm up for anything, once. Walking into people's lives. It's the only thing I really liked about being a journalist. Opening strange wardrobes, looking under beds.

ANDREW. Yes, it's great. You never get used to it, that feeling. It's all about people, I think. You must miss it.

REBECCA. Oh no, I've never been happier. Sitting alone in my room, writing books. Seeing you. With just an occasional treat. Like this. A quick look at the world of money and ambition.

LAMBERT LE ROUX *has entered and, unknown to them, is standing behind them.*

LE ROUX. You must be Andrew May.

There is a silence. LE ROUX *moves across and takes both of* ANDREW's *hands enfolding them like a bishop.* LE ROUX *looks straight in his eyes.*

ANDREW (*softly*). I'd begun to think I'd only ever meet you on the telephone.

LE ROUX. You don't need to meet the people you like.

ANDREW. Then why are you meeting me now?

LE ROUX. It's a sign of favour.

A smile between them.

LE ROUX. And you've brought Miss Foley with you. (*He takes her hand.*)

REBECCA. I didn't think you knew me.

LE ROUX. But I have your book, *A Child's Guide To The World*. I was hoping you'd sign it for me.

SYLVESTER *rushes on. His sleeves are rolled up. He has sheaves of paper and a huge, old fashioned ledger in his arms and is about to speak.* LE ROUX *waves him away.*

LE ROUX. Eaton, not now.

SYLVESTER *turns round and goes straight out again.*

ANDREW. I've brought today's paper.

LE ROUX. Ah thanks.

LE ROUX *takes the* Bystander *from* ANDREW. *He steps forward, feet apart, holding the paper at arms' length. He looks at the front page, turns it, looks at the back page, not reading and hands it back to* ANDREW.

LE ROUX. It's very good.

ANDREW. I'm afraid I've gone over to Garamond. Just for the headlines, of course. I wanted to check with you, but . . . Well, sometimes I'm not always able to . . . reach you.

LE ROUX. You have me now.

ANDREW. The figures are ridiculously flattering.

He offers a file which LE ROUX *accepts but does not open.*

The recent charge forward the *Bystander* has made is down to small ads. They've boomed because of the recession. As you saw. People have to sell all their things.

LE ROUX (*smiling, to* REBECCA). He talks himself down.

REBECCA. Yes he does. Don't you think it's an attractive characteristic?

LE ROUX. To me. And obviously to you.

ELLIOT FRUIT-NORTON *storms on to the stage in a fury, shouting.*

FRUIT-NORTON. This is absolutely intolerable! I have entered a private club!

A REPORTER *comes on.*

REPORTER. Just give me something, sir . . .

FRUIT-NORTON. I have absolutely nothing to add to my statement!

REBECCA. What is going on?

ANDREW. It's Elliot Fruit-Norton.

FRUIT-NORTON. Steward! Steward! Get this man thrown out.

REPORTER. Few lines, sir.

ANDREW. He's in trouble on the *Victory*.

FRUIT-NORTON *points at* ANDREW.

FRUIT-NORTON. You! Kindly throw this man out!

ANDREW. But I . . .

REPORTER. S'all right! S'all right! I'm on my way. Just doing a job.

The WAITER *arrives, with tray, on it two drinks and a sandwich on a plate.*

REPORTER. S'called reporting. Wouldn't know about that on the *Victory*. Too busy making up Latin quips, and jokes about golf. (*He goes off.*)

FRUIT-NORTON. The insufferable impertinence of journalists!

WAITER. Sir?

FRUIT-NORTON. Is there nowhere private any more? (*He goes off.*)

WAITER. Two spritzers. Cheese sandwich. (*He puts the drinks and the sandwich down. To* LE ROUX:) Do you want a drink, Sir?

ANDREW (*to* LE ROUX). Do you have any idea? Who the bidder for the *Victory* is?

There is a silence, the WAITER *in attendance.*

LE ROUX. No. I won't have a drink.

The WAITER *goes on his way with a whistle. A silence.*
LE ROUX *crosses the stage and stands on the other side.*

ANDREW. My God!

LE ROUX. You're surprised? Why? Why should it surprise you?

ANDREW. Well, for my . . . No. Will they ever . . .

LE ROUX. Ever let me in? Let me in? Let me in? (*He stares away.*) Moral feelings? They pass. A second. What are they? Little chemical drops in the brain. A vague feeling of unease, like indigestion. A physical mood. Too much dinner. 'Oh, I have a feeling', then in the morning it's gone. You're there. You're the owner. You're a fact. People adjust. The unthinkable yesterday becomes the way of things. New moral attitudes. New indigestion. It all passes. Pass and move on. (*A silence. Then he looks at the glasses.*) What's that you're drinking?

REBECCA. Spritzer.

LE ROUX (*smiles*). It's too early for me.

SYLVESTER *comes on fast.*

SYLVESTER. Lambert, we're going to have to talk before the meeting.

ANDREW. Do you want us to go?

LE ROUX. I'm seeing the Trustees at twelve o'clock.

ANDREW *looks at his watch.*

ANDREW. Well if you . . .

SYLVESTER. Their books are in the most incredible mess.

LE ROUX (*to* ANDREW). He only got them at six-thirty this morning.

SYLVESTER. We've never been told the extent of the damage. (*He holds the books out in the general direction of the other three.*) Look. There's three kinds of ink on every page. When we made our bid we didn't know the scale of the losses.

ANDREW. Have you already bought it?

LE ROUX. Oh no.

SYLVESTER. It's losing a million a week!

LE ROUX (*smiles*). Well then, they'll be all the more keen to sell it.

SYLVESTER. This newspaper that nobody reads. Whose circulation is spiralling downwards. That everyone says is as important as marmalade. It's losing fifty fucking million a year.

MICHAEL QUINCE *comes quickly into the room.*

QUINCE. They're here.

LE ROUX. All right.

QUINCE *goes out again.*

SYLVESTER. Do you want to look at these books?

LE ROUX (*shakes his head*). No, not now, the Trustees are coming. I've hired this famous room for a meeting. Andrew, I'd like you to stay. They're meeting to judge my suitability to be Proprietor of the *Victory*. In its highest traditions. You understand, I need a character reference. And you know me better than anyone else in this country.

REBECCA. He only met you today.

QUINCE *comes back on again quickly.*

QUINCE. The Chairman seems to be in favour of us. The Bishop of Putney is the one who is going mad.

At the back an old man in bishop's garb comes on, with white hair, bushy eyebrows and a bright pink and red face. He is waving in advance of coming into the room.

PUTNEY. Greetings, sinners, greetings!

QUINCE. My Lord Bishop.

LE ROUX (*to* ANDREW). I want you to be Editor of the *Victory*.

At once LE ROUX moves away upstage to where the BISHOP

is being introduced to SYLVESTER *by* QUINCE. ANDREW *is left open-mouthed downstage.*

LE ROUX. My Lord.

QUINCE. Do you two know each other?

PUTNEY. Hello. I'm Putney.

QUINCE. My Lord Bishop, this is Eaton Sylvester.

SYLVESTER. Hello, Bishop, how's it hanging?

SYLVESTER *glides away, the* BISHOP *puzzled by his remark.* ELLIOT FRUIT-NORTON *storms by him into the room. He is followed some paces behind by a much calmer figure,* LORD BEN SILK. *He is substantially over-weight, deeply suntanned and in a suit of the highest quality, dark blue with a Jermyn Street stripe.*

FRUIT-NORTON. I do not, I will not believe this. (*To* LE ROUX.) I'm sorry, I can't shake your hand.

SILK. I've just told him. (*He smiles at* LE ROUX. *He sits down and opens his briefcase at a low table in the middle of the room.*) As Chairman I hope we can do this as quickly as possible.

FRUIT-NORTON. The *Victory* sold to the owner of the *Tide.*

PUTNEY. Gentlemen, please, let's not prejudge the issue.

REBECCA. Andrew, did you hear that?

ANDREW. Editor? Me?

FRUIT-NORTON. Floodgates of filth.

LE ROUX. These are friends of mine.

SILK. I see. The position is this. The shares are on offer to Mr Le Roux's company. The sale itself cannot take place until the Trustees give their blessing. The criteria plainly set down in the deeds of the Trust are that the owner be — and I quote: 'a proper person', unquote. And that editorial independence be guaranteed. The purpose of this extraordinary meeting is to give Mr Le Roux a formal hearing, for us to make a balanced, sane, mature judgement, independent of party or personal whim. (*There is a pause. He turns.*) Bishop.

PUTNEY. Speaking for all the Trustees — Dame Elsa is presently on Rockall, and sent via Michael her proxy vote —

QUINCE *takes out a sealed envelope from his breast pocket.*

QUINCE. I have it here.

FRUIT-NORTON. This is outrageous.

QUINCE *opens the palms of his hands at FRUIT-NORTON across the room.*

SYLVESTER. It's in her writing.

PUTNEY. What most worries the Trustees is Mr Le Roux's record on apartheid.

LE ROUX (*smiles*). Something about the English. They're always obsessed with the past. (*He nods to SYLVESTER.*) Eaton . . .

SYLVESTER *has produced a British passport which he now shows round the room.*

SYLVESTER. Mr Le Roux is no longer a South African.

PUTNEY. Goodness.

SYLVESTER. We bought him one of these.

FRUIT-NORTON. Bought! A British passport!

SYLVESTER. Just out of politeness, we thought you'd be flattered. Mr Le Roux could choose any nationality he likes.

FRUIT-NORTON. Quince got you this, from the Home Secretary.

QUINCE. I resent that.

SYLVESTER. It's not true.

LE ROUX. Be assured I went through normal channels. Albeit at unusual speed.

SYLVESTER. I'd say.

LE ROUX (*his accent thickens*). I am 100 per cent English. No trace of my origins remains.

PUTNEY *is struggling to keep up with this.*

PUTNEY. But that doesn't mean . . .

LE ROUX. What?

PUTNEY. I mean you're technically English . . . But if you
remember the Free Council of Churches once published
a report about conditions for workers in South Africa. Your
factories were not exempted.

LE ROUX. Black worked beside Indian, to generate wealth. (*He
pauses and smiles. Very casually.*) Anyway what are you
suggesting? That I would persecute black journalists? Are
there any black journalists on the *Victory?* Elliot, you'd know.

FRUIT-NORTON. No. Well. I. Not. Precisely . . . At this
moment.

LE ROUX. There you are. The problem doesn't arise.

PUTNEY. No, hang about . . . er.

LE ROUX (*suddenly on the offensive*). I do hate this negative,
carping line of questioning.

SILK. Yes, I agree.

FRUIT-NORTON. I am not questioning, I am stating. Lambert
Le Roux is not a proper person.

LE ROUX (*quietly*). And what alternative would you suggest?

LE ROUX *smiles at* SYLVESTER, *then at* REBECCA.

SYLVESTER. Yeah.

SILK. This is not entirely relevent . . .

FRUIT-NORTON. As Lord Silk very well knows, we are in the
midst of forming a co-operative.

SILK. Oh God.

FRUIT-NORTON. Some of the most senior and experienced
journalists on the *Victory,* a number of them Fellows of All
Souls, who have decided the time has come to take their
lives into their own hands.

LE ROUX. I see. (*He smiles around the room.*) This is a very
interesting development. Have you heard this, Eaton?

SYLVESTER. Kindergarten. A lot of journos who've still got
their willies in their hands.

The BISHOP *of* PUTNEY *looks a little puzzled.*

LE ROUX. Well I must admit it had me somewhat confused.
Mr Fruit-Norton . . . *You* surely, an apostle of free enterprise!
Under your editorship the *Victory* has hardly blazed a trail for
workers control.

FRUIT-NORTON. No I . . .

LE ROUX. On the contrary, the market has been celebrated. I've
read your editorials. 'Healthy competition'? 'Stripped down'?
'Tooth and claw'? Why this sudden conversion to
communistical socialism?

FRUIT-NORTON. This is hardly . . .

LE ROUX (*to* SILK). What says ISD?

SILK. Well yes. Your idea, Elliot, though excellent in itself, is
unlikely to appeal to the parent company ISD. Who are,
after all, the owners of the *Victory*. We here are only the Trust
whose duty is to administer the sale.

LE ROUX. That's right.

SILK. International Song and Dance are themselves a classic
testimony to the success of entrepreneurial vigour. They
started in the thirties as a cabaret booking agency. They now
make the tail end of the F-16 bomber. I think we may say a
co-operative is unlikely to appeal.

FRUIT-NORTON *looks a little desperately around the room.*

FRUIT-NORTON. A new kind of co-operative. An unsocialist
co-operative, unhindered by egalitarian practices. A
co-operative with a small tightly-knit leadership.

LE ROUX. Gentlemen, I think we may be wasting our time.

FRUIT-NORTON *gets up.*

FRUIT-NORTON. You will not own it! You have not counted
on my most basic objections! This . . .

From papers on a table, he picks up a copy of the Tide,
waves it and throws it down.

PUTNEY. Oh is that today's *Tide*?

He picks it up and opens it, revealing one huge headline —
'BANG BANG TITTY TITTY BANG '.

FRUIT-NORTON. Are we really to say the man who produces this mulch, this pornography should be allowed to degrade the high standards of the *Victory*? (*To* PUTNEY:) Bishop, please.

PUTNEY *starts and puts the* Tide *down.*

FRUIT-NORTON. Oh of course I can see the people need a paper. In a sense, the *Tide* is well made. People who cannot articulate or reason — most people after all — most people that you meet on the street, or on the underground railway, who live in the prison of their own inadequacy, plainly they need a gay little jest every morning. And this at least the *Tide* is able to offer. It may even help them to develop their reading skills. Even in the shortest sentence one may find a noun, a verb, a predicate.

SYLVESTER. Yeah. Great.

FRUIT-NORTON. But I find it impossible to believe that the pedlar of this ranting, nipple-ridden broadsheet should be a man of sufficient distinction to run the *Victory*. He does not belong to the intellectual first division.

SILK. Elliot, you're going too far . . .

SYLVESTER. He's being bloody rude.

LE ROUX *is smiling, still very quiet.*

LE ROUX. Not rude, but confused. Surely the intellect on the paper is meant to be supplied by the editor.

FRUIT-NORTON. Well yes, of course. Certainly in my case. The leading first in Greats of my decade.

LE ROUX. I put the money up, that's all.

FRUIT-NORTON. But what guarantees that you won't interfere with the paper?

SILK. This is important.

LE ROUX *makes a little gesture towards* ANDREW.

LE ROUX. Andrew?

ANDREW. What? Oh I see. Oh well. You mean my experience?

FRUIT-NORTON. Who is this?

SYLVESTER. The Editor of *The Leicester Bystander*.

ANDREW. My experience is that he leaves you alone.

A long pause. They are all looking at ANDREW.

LE ROUX. Go on.

REBECCA. Andrew . . .

ANDREW. No, I mean I . . . Looking back on the period of my
editorship has been marked . . . (*He hesitates slightly.*) . . . by a
marked increase in sales. Up 12.7 — thanks to my community
policy, which I have been left at liberty to pursue. Mr Le Roux
operates on what I think is called the arms-length principle.
You are aware he is a man you are very keen to please. He is
there, present in the building, without seeming to visit
it at all. Any major change of policy — for instance I
removed a page of news and replaced it with small . . . (*He
hesitates again.*) inter-community messages — well I at once
got a telex from Mr Le Roux in Geneva thanking me. I think
it boils down to a question of trust. (*He looks round the room,
his confidence growing.*) I can see it's important to you that
these things be defined by guidelines. Exact areas of power
laid down. Of course. Yes. They must be in print. Agreed.
Legislated, if you like. But what is truly important is the
spirit. It has to be trust. For fiteen months I have been
trusted.

There is a moment's pause.

SILK. Bishop?

PUTNEY. Yes I'm impressed.

LE ROUX. Elliot?

FRUIT-NORTON. Yes. Well. The boy is here. I must accept his
deposition.

ANDREW. No it's not, it's just what I think.

LE ROUX. Given what Mr May said, I can see that, should the sale go through, you will hardly wish to serve as my editor.

There is a very long silence.

FRUIT-NORTON. I think that's a separate question, you will find.

LE ROUX (*to* FRUIT-NORTON). Meaning?

FRUIT-NORTON. Whoever buys the paper, I of course intend to carry on.

LE ROUX (*nods a moment*). That essential relationship of trust, from what you have said about me and my papers, does not exist between us.

FRUIT-NORTON. Please. I am sure . . . We can start to build one from here.

There is a silence. Everyone is embarrassed by
FRUIT-NORTON.

SILK. Elliot, I think for your own sake it would be unwise to say any more.

SYLVESTER. Too right.

SILK. Any incoming proprietor would want to appoint his own man.

FRUIT-NORTON. Ben, are you saying you're going to let me go? The Trust is meant to protect me, you promised to protect me.

SILK. Elliot, it's not up to me. But I've wanted to warn you there has been a drift. Your obsessional articles on supply-side economics have hardly boosted circulation. No one can understand them. The one man I've met who could says they are wholly inaccurate.

FRUIT-NORTON *stands, his cause lost.*

LE ROUX (*chipper*). I shall print on the *Tide's* presses, thus halving costs at a stroke.

FRUIT-NORTON. You mean you're giving it away? To this mendicant? With no guarantees?

LE ROUX. Absolute guarantees. What guarantees would you like?

SILK. The fundamental guarantee, editorial independence.

LE ROUX. Of course. I will have nothing to do with the daily running of the paper.

SILK. Accepted. Yes? With alacrity.

LE ROUX. Absolute editorial freedom. The right of the editor to appoint his own people. The right of the editor to appeal to the Trust.

SILK. This is excellent.

SYLVESTER. Copper-bottomed legal guarantees, drawn up kosher.

LE ROUX. I would also suggest, in the spirit of this agreement, should it go through, that we build in one essential safeguard. A weekly visit to the newsroom by the Bishop of Putney. To conduct a short prayer meeting.

SILK. Brilliant.

PUTNEY. A most imaginative suggestion.

LE ROUX. And one that will give a regular physical expression to the exact value of this agreement.

They all get up, led by LE ROUX. FRUIT-NORTON *makes a strange strangled noise.*

LE ROUX. What's the matter, Elliot? Aren't you a Christian?

SILK. The terms are ideal.

FRUIT-NORTON. Open the doors, why not? Just give away the old family silver. The Barbarians are here, give them everything, why not? (*He goes out.*)

LE ROUX. The first thing will be to stem the losses. I'll speak to the unions tonight.

SYLVESTER. Six o'clock?

LE ROUX. Fine.

PUTNEY. Oh you think . . . ?

LE ROUX. What?

PUTNEY. Already?

LE ROUX. We just agreed it. It's over. Am I right, Ben? Have I misread the meeting?

SILK. Not at all.

SYLVESTER. We'll need an interim period. Shut the paper down for three days. Till we've squared the unions.

SILK (*impishly*). Good luck.

LE ROUX *is heading for the door.*

ANDREW. Oh er . . .

LE ROUX *turns.*

LE ROUX. I've booked you all a table at Maxim's.

PUTNEY. Oh how marvellous.

SILK. Thanks.

LE ROUX. No, you go. Enjoy yourselves. I'm paying. I'm not coming, it's my children's sports day. (*And suddenly he has gone.*)

SYLVESTER. The table's in my name. (*And he has gone.*)

SILK. Well, there we are. That's . . .

PUTNEY. Gosh.

SILK. That was excellent.

A pause, they are dazed.

PUTNEY. Yes, it's refreshing, don't you think?

SILK. Good. Well, it's lunch. (*He is gathering up his papers.*) I like eating, I like sleeping, but most of all I like chairing a satisfactory meeting.

QUINCE. Nobody does it better than you, Ben.

SILK. That's right.

PUTNEY. Well done. It's a Christian thing. (PUTNEY *looks vaguely at* ANDREW.) Are you . . . ?

QUINCE. My car, my driver.

PUTNEY *turns and joins* QUINCE *and* SILK *as they go out.*

PUTNEY. I have to be in Lambeth at three.

They've gone. REBECCA *and* ANDREW *are left alone on the stage.*

ANDREW. Did that include us? At Maxim's? Were we meant to go?

REBECCA *looks across at him, not answering.*

Before the meeting, did he ask me to be editor?

REBECCA. He mentioned it, yes, and then he moved on. He's classy. It's brilliant technique. Charm is so unfair.

ANDREW. What are you saying? You don't want me to take it?

REBECCA. No of course. Are you serious? You must. I'd like to come along too.

ANDREW. What do you mean?

REBECCA. Hire me. I'll join you. If you make me a promise.

ANDREW. What kind?

REBECCA. A test. Some test of when it's got to you.

ANDREW. It won't get to me. Look — I'm here, I'm alive. In the Irving Club. It costs me nothing, it's a job, I'm not touched. See? (*He raises a finger.*) Move that headline. Crop that picture. Go to seven columns. See, I can do it. That's my talent. Not all this business of shouting in rooms.

REBECCA. Promise me you'll never tell the same lie three times.

ANDREW. In a week?

REBECCA. In a day. The same lie three times a day. You promise?

ANDREW. Yes. I promise.

REBECCA. Three times and I leave you.

He smiles. They look at each other, in love.

Scene Five

The stage is prepared for the fifth scene, as ELLIOT FRUIT-NORTON *comes to the front of the stage to be interviewed for the last time by hectoring* REPORTERS. *Meanwhile the Irving Club disappears.*

REPORTERS. ⎫   Elliot! Elliot! Mr Fruit-Norton! Look at
PHOTOGRAPHERS. ⎬   me! Look at me!

FIRST REPORTER. What are your compensation terms, Mr Fruit-Norton?

SECOND. How much are you getting?

FIRST. Is it true they've given you a life subscription to the *Victory?*

FRUIT-NORTON *stops. Flash guns, microphones.*

FRUIT-NORTON. Please. I have today terminated my employment.

SECOND. Were you pushed?

FRUIT-NORTON. Please — after eight happy years as Editor, it is indeed hard to imagine the paper without me, and I know my colleagues share this feeling.

FIRST. What are you going to do now?

SECOND. Down the job centre, Elliot?

FRUIT-NORTON. Viewed in the evening light of history, my tenure at the *Victory* may seem only a passing shadow. But the unique qualities of civilisation which I have sought to advance are sempi-ternal. Addison, Steele, Johnson. These have been my constant companions, and as I retire now to spend time with my wife Gilda, my animals and my two strapping lads, I know that friendly ghosts of the great journalists will join us for dinner at our Suffolk home in Much Blakeley.

SECOND. What are you going to do?

FRUIT-NORTON. I have accepted the Chairmanship of the National Greyhound Racetrack Inspection Board. A role to which I shall bring the same qualities of discrimination, balance and probity which have characterised my time at the *Victory.* Thank you gentlemen.

FRUIT-NORTON *sweeps off pursued, the gaggle following him shouting.*

REPORTERS. Greyhounds, Mr Fruit-Norton?

NEWSVENDORS *cross the stage.*

FIRST NEWSVENDOR. EDITOR GOES TO THE DOGS!

SECOND. FRUIT-NORTON: I'LL BRING CLASS TO DOG-TRACK!

THIRD. SNOB MOVES IN: PUNTERS NIGHTMARE!

FIRST. SPRINGBOK BUYER TAKES OVER TODAY.

Meanwhile behind them the newsroom of the Victory *has been assembled. It is of modern design. Two lines of desks stretch away into the distance like a maze. They are piled with typewriters, papers, files, reference books, telephones. At the very centre of the stage LE ROUX is standing, in a pile of newspapers and shouting at the top of his voice. All round the working area are many JOURNALISTS who are frantically scurrying around, pushing into each other. Telephones are ringing loudly and being answered in a spirit of open panic.*

LE ROUX. What the fuck is happening? What the fuck is going on here? Christ I've never read such a load of fucking shit! (*He shakes the paper angrily in his hand.*) It's shit! It's shit! What a load of fucking shit! God who writes this fucking rubbish? (*He tears the paper into shreds and points at a* JOURNALIST.) You! What do you do?

FIRST JOURNALIST. Home Affairs, sir.

LE ROUX. Eaton? Where are you?

SYLVESTER *glides onto the stage at great speed, papers in hand, sleeves rolled up, a smile on his face.*

How much have we spent?

SYLVESTER. A hundred and fifty thousand.

LE ROUX. How much does that leave in the firing fund?

SYLVESTER. *Three* hundred and fifty thousand.

LE ROUX turns back to the FIRST JOURNALIST.

LE ROUX. You're fired.

SYLVESTER. Upstairs!

LE ROUX is now staring at a shred of newspaper in his hand.

LE ROUX. Who wrote this article on Central American politics? Who is it? Is it anybody here? Put your hand up.

A nervous JOURNALIST *raises a hand.*

Sack yourself please. Spare me the embarrassment. No gringo should have to read this kind of stuff.

A THIRD JOURNALIST is trying to sneak out. LE ROUX whirls round.

You. Where are you going?

THIRD JOURNALIST. I'm going to the lavatory.

LE ROUX. Use a public toilet. You're fired.

SYLVESTER smiles at the THIRD JOURNALIST *and points as he passes.*

SYLVESTER. The accountant's on the fourth floor.

On the other side of the stage a FOURTH JOURNALIST, doubled over, is trying not to be seen.

LE ROUX. Which are you? Have I fired you?

FOURTH JOURNALIST. No sir . . .

LE ROUX. Then get over there. Get over that side. All the ones I haven't fired are over that side. Don't confuse me. Have a cup of coffee. Where is marketing? They are the worst.

A FIFTH JOURNALIST, who has just entered the newsroom, freezes in horror, turns and runs off. LE ROUX has picked up a double crown poster which is an advertisement for the paper.

What is this slogan? 'THE VICTORY IS YOURS'? What does it mean? What is this, communistic propaganda? All the advertising people must go. (*He turns to SYLVESTER and shouts with increased savagery.*) Don't even let them take a pencil with them! Search them! Let them go out naked!

A nervous younger man, with prematurely grey hair has now approached. He has a clipboard under his arm. He is very thin, almost emaciated. His pin-stripe suit hangs loosely on him.

WHICKER-BASKETT. Excuse me Sir. I am the Deputy Editor. I've been holding the fort. I trust you find everything to your satisfaction.

LE ROUX. And what is your name?

WHICKER-BASKETT. My name is Cliveden Whicker-Baskett.

LE ROUX. In South Africa there are no men called Whicker-Baskett. The name is totally unknown. And who is this? (LE ROUX *points with his toe at a body which is lying under a desk. He kicks him.*)

WHICKER-BASKETT. Oh. That's Mack Wellington. The drama critic. 'Whipper' Wellington. He's just been to a lunch-time theatre.

Drunkenly the man rises up from beneath the desk. LE ROUX *looks down without a flicker.*

LE ROUX. What sort of criteria do you use in your reviews? Is it more important that the play flatters your personal prejudices, or do you make a genuine attempt at objectivity?

'WHIPPER' (*groans*). Oh God.

He blacks out. As he falls ANDREW, REBECCA *and* BILL SMILEY *come on. The two men are in a satirical version of morning dress, with top hats and decadent button holes. They are holding champagne bottles and have confetti all over them.* REBECCA *as a joke, is wearing a bridal veil and a startlingly attractive dress. They stop in mid-celebration, bottles raised.* LE ROUX *turns. He speaks quietly.*

LE ROUX. Andrew. And where have you been?

ANDREW (*trying not to slur his speech*). Oh gosh. I know. I'm sorry. It's my first day and I should have been here.

LE ROUX. Indeed.

ANDREW. But I just had this silly idea that before I started . . .

REBECCA. We decided to get married.

A silence. No one dares to move.

LE ROUX. And how was it?

ANDREW. Oh it went very well.

Everyone waits for LE ROUX's *reaction. He turns. A couple of people instinctively duck finding themselves in his eye-line.* SYLVESTER *stands smiling at the back.* LE ROUX *points at* ANDREW *and addresses the whole room.*

LE ROUX. This man is unique. You are lucky men. He has a sense of humour. This is something I admire. Please, all of you, try and acquire a sense of humour. (*To* ANDREW.) Who is this with you?

BILL. Bill Smiley. I'm the best man.

LE ROUX. Are you a journalist?

BILL. Yes, actually.

LE ROUX. You're hired.

BILL. No you can't fire me, I don't work for you . . .

LE ROUX. No not *fired, hired.* (LE ROUX *turns back to address the petrified* JOURNALISTS.) You see, witty man. (*To* BILL:) I have many vacancies. Go and find any job you like. (*He turns to* WHICKER-BASKETT, *almost melancholy.*) Whicker-Baskett, did I sack you?

WHICKER-BASKETT. Oh. No.

LE ROUX. What difference does it make? I'm sacking you now.

SYLVESTER. This is magnificent. I've worked years for Lambert and the reward is moments like this.

Unnoticed by LE ROUX *one of the three* JOURNALISTS *makes a dash to the safe side of the room where he is greeted by his colleagues.* LE ROUX *then turns, shaking off his melancholy.*

LE ROUX. We have cast out the bad. There was bad on this

paper. Life is a fight between the good and the bad. We all of us may now work in a warm and friendly atmosphere. Let's make a good, a lovely paper, a family paper full of love. On this wedding day, no more unpleasantness.

There is a pause.

Right everyone. Let's get the news on the street.

ACT TWO

Scene One

The newsroom of the Victory. *It is nine o'clock. The first edition is due in fifteen minutes. There is a calm and orderly atmosphere. Various journalists are sitting working at their desks or filing copy.*

At the centre of the room sits DOUG FANTOM, *the Night Editor. He is a man in his forties, wiry, tough, with shirt sleeves rolled up.*

A JOURNALIST *passes through the newsroom with sheaves of paper.*

JOURNALIST. Last copy please. First edition due in fifteen minutes.

A JOURNALIST *yawns.* DOUG FANTOM *is sitting back with his legs on the desk reading some copy. At the side* LARRY PUNT, *a nervous young reporter, is sneaking glances at him. When* FANTOM *eventually speaks it is to himself.*

FANTOM. For my sins, for my sins. (*He calls out.*) Whose is this?

LARRY approaches at once.

LARRY. Oh it's mine.

FANTOM. It's a very nice story, Larry. Well done.

LARRY. Thank you.

FANTOM. Have you been to Loch Fergus?

LARRY. Well . . . yes, Mr Fantom. I was there just after it happened. Doesn't that show?

FANTOM. Let's see, let's read this out.

Without comment he hands the copy to LARRY.

LARRY. 'Women who have recently formed a peace camp on Loch Fergus where the building of the new Fork Lightning missile is soon to begin, were yesterday recovering from a surprise attack by two hundred policemen.

'The police mounted their attack at night in full riot gear and destroyed the camp in twenty-five minutes. Twenty-seven women were charged with various alleged minor offences and subsequently spent the night in cells at Loch Fergus police station.

'Commenting on the surprise attack Mrs Mary Kingham, a thirty-four-year-old mother of two, said "I was dragged by the hair from my sleeping bag. I was thrown violently into the back of a van while being abused by a masked policeman".

'Last night two women were still being detained with serious injuries in Loch Fergus General Hospital'.

FANTOM (*nods judiciously*). Yes, well, that's good, that makes things very clear.

LARRY. Thank you.

FANTOM. The first rule of reporting: to distinguish between what's been told to you and what you actually saw. Did you actually see them being pulled by the hair?

LARRY. No. But I did meet the woman. There was blood. The hair had been torn away from the scalp.

FANTOM. Yes. To be supercilious, Larry, a woman of that type . . . It is possible she tore her own hair out.

LARRY. Yes. And kicked herself in the groin.

FANTOM. Quite.

The two men look at each other without humour. There is a short silence.

This is just a professional exercise. To maintain standards, that's all.

LARRY *hands the copy back to him, silently.* FANTOM *puts it on the desk in front of him and takes a Mont Blanc fountain pen.*

Women. What sort of women? (*He writes.*) Middle-aged women. Peace. Camp. Peace on this paper is always in inverted commas. You'll find that in the style book. Peace *camp.* Camp? Camp implies facilities, showers, toilets, camps are things you take the family to in Brittany. Call it a peace — inverted commas — squat. Better. 'Middle-aged women who squatted illegally . . .' Better. Do police really 'Mount an attack'? Surely they're defending *us*? Society? Themselves? So it's 'Police defending themselves'. (*He makes a great mark across the paper.*) 'Destroyed'? No. Cleared the site. In twenty-five minutes . . . that's 'Quickly and efficiently'. This Mary Kingham. Do we know she's still with her husband? Left her children I suppose, to squat all over the road.

LARRY. There's no proof of that.

FANTOM. No. Abused by a what? (*He smiles up at* LARRY *good-naturedly.*) Quote 'A masked policeman'? What is this, South America, Larry? (*He scores a line through the paper.*) The piece is too long. OK. Well done, Larry. You're coming along.

He holds the piece of paper above his head and a passing journalist takes it from him and goes off.

LARRY. Pravda.

FANTOM. You what?

LARRY *moves away.* FANTOM *swings back to his typewriter in his swivel chair. A* JOURNALIST *calls out to a colleague.*

FIRST JOURNALIST. Mike! Make sure you don't miss *News At Ten*.

SECOND JOURNALIST. Sure thing. I'll copy it down and call it the *Victory*.

Office joke. Everyone laughs. From the back there is a voice.

ANDREW (*off*). Yeah, like we do every night.

ANDREW MAY *sweeps on to the stage in evening dress, a coat draped over his shoulders. At once there is applause. Most of the* JOURNALISTS *stand and shake him by the hand. He is carrying a large brass maquette of a bent forefinger.*

Everyone, it's ours, we've won it.

ALL. Oh well done, well done.

ANDREW. Here it is.

Without moving from his chair, FANTOM *holds out a hand.*

FANTOM. Congratulations.

A JOURNALIST. Can't go higher.

ANDREW. The Golden Typing Finger. Editor of the Year.

ALL. That's marvellous. Congratulations.

FANTOM. Can't go higher.

ANDREW. I told them, at the presentation . . . this isn't just for me. In a very real sense, this finger is for all of you.

He holds the Golden Finger up and there is a flash as he is photographed, surrounded by his colleagues.

Everyone has been so warm and loyal, to help me find my feet in this job.

A JOURNALIST. I'd just like to say on behalf of all of us, this is the best bloody and most wonderful editor most of us have had the privilege to slave for and if ever a man deserved a professional gong it's Andrew May.

Applause.

ANDREW. Business as usual. We won this for being a professional newspaper. Well done everyone. And now on we go.

A couple of people pat him on the back. BILL SMILEY has come on, also in evening dress.

BILL. Aren't you coming up?

ANDREW. Yes. Just a minute. (*To a* JOURNALIST.) Lambert is having a celebration dinner upstairs.

A JOURNALIST. Sounds lovely.

ANDREW. Yes. This has been such a perfect day. I rather want to see the paper to bed.

BILL has gone back to his desk to check over his work. Everyone else is also working. ANDREW is left standing for a moment, a little lost, looking for something to do.

FANTOM. We had a call from Downing street.

ANDREW. Oh. Oh really?

FANTOM. Nothing serious. Grade three bollocking. There was a piece in the Business News yesterday, we somehow seemed to say that the pound was weak.

ANDREW. Oh God.

FANTOM. Yes, I know. Look . . . (*He holds out a sheet of paper.*) I've got a piece correcting it. The pound isn't weak, the dollar is strong.

ANDREW. Ah well, that should . . .

FANTOM. Yes it will.

He nods hopefully. FANTOM *goes back to work.* ANDREW *turns, absently.*

JACK 'BREAKER' BOND *enters. A large, bullishly tough, working-class man. He is in evening dress and smokes a cigar.*

BREAKER. Good evening chief. Great news.

ANDREW. Thank you, Breaker.

BREAKER. Can I see it?

ANDREW *shows him the Golden Finger.*

Very nice. Brings credit to us all. I'll make my speech. As Branch Secretary of the Union and Father of the Chapel and and and and.

ANDREW. You must be going up to the dinner.

BREAKER. Too right. Wouldn't miss it. Royal guests, I hear. I love meeting 'em. I've met nearly all of 'em. I'm a real castle creeper. By the way, did I mention you may be 'aving a bit o' trouble tonight?

ANDREW. Oh no Breaker, please . . .

FANTON. Do we know about this?

BREAKER. Yeah, pity in't it? With a royal guest in the boardroom. Pity not to get your paper out.

ANDREW. Is there any danger of that?

BREAKER. No, well, at the moment the lads are holding a meeting to discuss the new technology . . . All those junk TV's we got in the back of the building. All with sort of green screens. And the plugs missing.

ANDREW. How long will that take?

BREAKER. The machines have been left temporarily unsupervised. And also on. Which can lead to some nasty mechanical problems.

ANDREW. Breaker, what possibly . . . (*He checks, calms himself.*) What do you want? What can it be? (*He looks around, appealing for support.*) Mr Le Roux has done everything. We gave you everything.

BREAKER. Same old chestnut, Andrew. Pay and conditions. They never seem to quite measure up.

FANTOM (*quietly*). No.

BREAKER. I mean I love this paper, as you know. The *Victory*. Great English newspaper. On the other 'and, put it another way, it's all such shit you're writing why shouldn't a few working men make two grand a week? I mean that way the paper does *some* good.

ANDREW. Breaker, please . . .

BREAKER. Hear me out Andrew. I mean if there were anything *in* the paper, like a bit of good writing now and then, we'd roll up our sleeves and help you. Now and then. But at the moment this is not on. Eh, Doug?

FANTOM. It's never been on, has it Breaker?

BREAKER. In this business, you make your own luck.

There is a sudden silence in the newsroom. Everyone is listening. Then BREAKER moves across, all eyes on him and pats FANTOM on the back. Then BREAKER turns to ANDREW.

BREAKER. I'll go upstairs, I'll have a word with Lambert.

ANDREW. Would you, Breaker? I'd be very grateful.

BREAKER. Yes. Lambert understands us.

There is a complete silence in the newsroom. REBECCA has silently entered. She is wearing a mackintosh and carrying a foolscap envelope.

Looks like your wife has arrived.

He turns and goes out in silence.

REBECCA. What's going on?

ANDREW. Right. Back to work everyone. (*To* DOUG:) Do you think it's all right?

FANTOM. It's fine.

ANDREW *turns to explain to* REBECCA.

ANDREW. We had a visit from Breaker. He's on very good form. Where have you been? I thought you were coming to the presentation.

REBECCA. I was, Andrew. Then an old family friend of mine rang.

She looks him straight in the eye. Then slightly gestures with the foolscap envelope she is carrying. There is something in her voice that makes ANDREW *understand at once.*

ANDREW. What's that?

REBECCA. Well that's it. It's for us. It's a document. Secured from the Ministry of Defence.

ANDREW. I see. (*He pauses a moment, then turns.*) Doug?

REBECCA. Hold on. I don't want Doug.

ANDREW. You can trust Doug. He's been here for years.

REBECCA. That's what I mean.

DOUG *swivels in his chair.*

FANTOM. What is it?

REBECCA. It's a document. It was given to me . . . got to me by somebody, I'm not saying who. By someone in the Ministry of Defence.

FANTOM. Yes.

REBECCA. It's classified.

FANTOM. Yes, well it would be.

REBECCA (*frowns*). Andrew, I think we should go and discuss this by ourselves. In your office.

ANDREW. Rebecca. This is a newspaper. I am Editor. Doug is Night Editor. You are an employee.

FANTOM. Please Rebecca you mistake my manner. Go on.

There is a pause.

REBECCA. Plutonium is carried . . .

ANDREW. Oh God . . .

REBECCA. . . . from nuclear power stations to Ministry of Defence establishments in flasks. The Minister has repeatedly asserted that these flasks are safe when dropped at heights of up to fifteen metres on to concrete or solid steel. The results of an internal Ministry testing programme show that flasks when dropped from twenty metres, can in fact leak. Do leak. As the Minister knows. As the Minister has known at the time of his three specific House of Commons denials. He's denied that such tests have ever taken place.

FANTOM. I see.

There is a pause.

Did you say who your source was?

REBECCA. No.

FANTOM. A friend of yours. A woman?

REBECCA *opens the envelope.*

REBECCA. This is it. The report. There's also a memo instructing civil servants to deny the existence of these tests, and obviously, therefore, not to disclose the results.

ANDREW. Yes. I see. Right. Yes. (*He turns.*) Oh my God it's happening.

FANTOM. Will you let me see?

REBECCA *hands the document to* FANTOM.

ANDREW. We've got one at last. Let me think. We've discussed this. With lawyers. We agreed a procedure. For exactly this eventuality. Now, what was it?

REBECCA. Don't be silly, Andrew, I've got to write it up now.

ANDREW. Yes, of course. No question. Certainly. Indeed. But first I'll obviously have to check that the documents are genuine . . .

REBECCA. Well, of course if *I* gave them to you . . .

FANTOM. They're genuine, yes. Look . . . (*He holds the papers up.*) The Minister's initials. Like little eels. I know his handwriting. I was up at Oxford with him.

ANDREW. Then in that case we must do our own authentication. Get the science right. Is our science man in? If we got him, Bill . . .

He calls out to BILL, *who gets up and comes over.*

REBECCA. What for? What d'you need him for?

BILL. What's happening?

ANDREW. He could check the scientific side. We'll need charts, diagrams, good strong graphics. Little explosions.

REBECCA. What's the point? The science is conclusive. It's all been done by Ministry officials.

ANDREW. Maybe we should do our own tests. Check the conclusions.

REBECCA. What, you mean drop a bomb in the newsroom?

ANDREW. No, I mean just, well . . . maintain professional standards! We're a professional newspaper. We stand by what we write. We validate conclusions.

REBECCA. Why? That's not what it's about.

FANTOM. Your wife understands. It's nothing to do with science, or nuclear fuels, or safety. It's politics.

REBECCA. Yes.

There is a silence. FANTOM *hands the document to* BILL SMILEY.

The Minister lied.

ANDREW. Yes, that's the angle I'm most worried about. Let's

face it, the Government'd go mad. They'd go for me. There's a fair chance they'd actually take me to court.

REBECCA. So?

ANDREW. Also, let's face it, there's the ethical question. Someone has stolen this document. We must think about ethics. The law. What they'd do to me. I could end up in gaol.

REBECCA. Well, wouldn't it be worth it?

ANDREW. Yes, but there is a real problem. If we break the law. This paper supports the law.

REBECCA. Does it support lying?

ANDREW. I'm not sure, I need some professional advice.

BILL *who has been reading the document, suddenly starts shouting and jumping about.*

BILL. Oh god, this is fantastic! Pay-gold at last! The ladder to heaven! Ten fucking years I've spent in the saltmines of this profession, doorstepping drunken councillors, and finally something that's real! And magnificent! That's not about traffic, or councils, or weddings! The joy of finally holding their balls in my hands! I'm so happy, oh God, let me do it, please let me do this one . . . .

ANDREW. Bill please, just let me think . . .

REBECCA. Why is it when you present the free press with a real opportunity, freedom is on the one hand a principle, and on the fucking other, in this case, doesn't apply.

ANDREW. I haven't decided! Just give me time . . .

LEANDER SCROOP *has appeared in the newsroom. A strikingly tall dandy, in evening dress and an opera cloak, he is carrying a small, personal hamper and an opera programme.*

SCROOP. My God. I have never had to witness such total desecration.

ANDREW. Leander. Now a lobby correspondent *would* be worth talking to.

SCROOP. Hiroshima!

ANDREW. He'll tell us how to handle it.

REBECCA. You don't have to handle it.

SCROOP. An outrage! An act of inhumanity! I shall bring it up at the board.

ANDREW. Good evening, Leander.

SCROOP *comes over to join them.*

SCROOP. I have been to see *Don Giovanni* at the Garden. Directed by some stone-faced Albanian. I can only tell you: Donna Elvira wore pebble glasses. 'Della Sua Pace' was sung from the barrel of a tank.

FANTOM. It sounds as if you have the makings of a piece. One of your long ones.

Unnoticed, FANTOM *slips out of the newsroom.*

ANDREW. Leander, we need your help. We have a big story. A classified document.

SCROOP. Ah yes. Which one?

ANDREW. What do you mean, which one?

SCROOP. Well I suppose inevitably it's from the Ministry of Defence.

ANDREW. Yes.

BILL. How do you know this?

SCROOP. I imagined you hacks would get a sniff of something eventually. If it's plutonium. Are we talking plutonium?

There is a pause.

BILL. You mean you already know?

ANDREW. Leander, what happened?

SCROOP. I heard of some document's existence. I spoke to the Minister. He was kind enough to clarify the story, to explain it from his point of view. One flask did crack, once.

BILL. And you did nothing? You just accepted it?

SCROOP. Certainly. Bear in mind he briefed me in the Lobby. The Lobby has rules. I met with the Minister. He was, in a sense, downing pink gins in Annie's bar. But officially he never drank anything. Officially no briefing occurred.

BILL. For God's sake, Leander . . .

SCROOP. He told me everything, therefore he told me nothing. A perfect English arrangement. Everything that happened did not happen. I was present at a meeting at which no one met. The only way you can have the confidence of Ministers is to have the confidence never to repeat what Ministers say.

REBECCA. My God, I think I'm going crazy.

ANDREW. Leander, which comes first? The Government or the paper?

SCROOP. This is all irrelevent. It's deeply unprofessional. There's no reason to discuss it. We have a policy. We are not bleeding hearts. We are not *The Daily Usurper*. We do not pitch our tents in the gutter. This paper never prints leaks.

REBECCA. *What?*

BILL. Leander from *you*!

SCROOP. Yes?

BILL. What was that story you had last week?

REBECCA. It stank.

SCROOP. I defend it.

ANDREW. Don't, please.

BILL. That clever little insinuation about the spread of herpes in the Labour HQ in the Walworth Road?

SCROOP. That wasn't a leak, that was a Government briefing.

BILL (*furious*). And there's a difference?

SCROOP. Of course. (SCROOP *looks at him.*) If you want news there are channels, there are means. 'Phone calls. Lunch at the Irving. A properly protected professional procedure. We can't have any Tom, Dick or Harry handling news. I mean this . . . (*He suddenly loses his temper.*) Who brought us this?

REBECCA. I did.

SCROOP. And who gave it to you? Some little sewer rat who imagines his own neurotic opinions should be weighed in the scale against matters of state. This is the disease of our times.

ANDREW is suddenly firm.

ANDREW. Leander, I'm lost. We're journalists, there's a story, that's all. I'll be judged by this decision. For ever. People will say 'Oh that night he put himself on the line. He published'.

They look at him.

Yes. And that's what I'm going to do. If you stop and think 'I won't use this story because I'll lose my access to power', you just become the Government's notice board on which they can pin anything they like. In return for what? What's in it for you, Leander? A Fleet Street knighthood? The royal bread knife? 'Arise, Sir Leander'?

SCROOP. How dare you?

ANDREW. I'm sorry, Leander. But you've really let us down. (*He picks up the document and throws it across the room to* BILL.) Bill, mark it up. I'm printing this document in its whole entirety. Every word. Scrap the feature pages. Front page lead story. Hold the presses. And you, Leander . . .

SCROOP. Yes?

ANDREW. You are . . .

There is a pause.

SCROOP. What am I?

ANDREW. F — fired.

SCROOP. Really? Is that in your gift?

LE ROUX is suddenly there at the back of the room with MICHAEL QUINCE *beside him. They are in evening dress.* DOUG FANTOM *is a few paces behind. The whole newsroom suddenly stops work.*

LE ROUX. What is this? I'm not even on to my pudding. I interrupt the royal train. A most amusing anecdote about hounds. We are about to put our spoons into the spun sugar of the commemorative *îles flottantes* and I am told I am needed downstairs. Behind her gracious smile, Her Highness was deeply pissed off.

ANDREW. Who sent for you?

FANTOM. I decided the proprietor would focus the discussion.

REBECCA. Andrew, I told you . . .

ANDREW. No, fair enough. I have nothing to hide.

He turns to LE ROUX.

LE ROUX. Back to work everyone. (*He moves through the room to* ANDREW.) You've decided to publish.

ANDREW. Yes. I stand by my decision.

LE ROUX. Good. I expect that from you, Andrew.

QUINCE (*to* ANDREW). I think I should warn you. Publication would be very unwise.

LE ROUX *holds up a hand.*

LE ROUX. Please. Let him speak. This is very interesting.

ANDREW. First thing tomorrow we'll go into conference with our lawyers, Rubbentrop, Pond and Salmon. We have a watertight defence.

LE ROUX. Good. Good.

ANDREW. Under Section Ten of the Contempt Act. A newspaper is legally entitled to protect its souces.

QUINCE. Except in case of National Security, for fucksake!

ANDREW. In this case I don't think that really applies.

QUINCE. Oh, you don't?

ANDREW. No. I see this as an issue of public safety. And political morality.

QUINCE. You fucking idiot, it's plutonium for bombs!

LE ROUX (*smiling*). It's a point, Andrew.

REBECCA. For God's sake don't go back, just print it. Expose the Minister of Defence as a liar. Kick him out of office.

LE ROUX. Heady stuff.

FANTOM. I don't think you'll find it as simple as that.

QUINCE. And what are you saying? When the High Court orders you to return this stolen document, you are actually planning what, to refuse?

REBECCA. Destroy it. That way they can't get you. Just light a cigarette.

ANDREW. Have a fire.

REBECCA. Be blithe.

ANDREW. Have some fun.

QUINCE. I thought on this paper we respected the law.

ANDREW. Well . . .

QUINCE. My own column, 'A View From The Garden', has consistently argued that the law is above all. Inexorable, beautiful, harsh, even-handed, absolute. The law in all its majesty, its icy splendour, the sun shining behind the mountain top of justice. British justice.

LE ROUX. Thank you, Michael.

QUINCE. I feel strongly about this. I was beaten at school.

ANDREW *has turned, confidently.*

ANDREW. And what can they do? They can't take it from us by force. All they can do is fine us. Money. Just money. Heavy punitive fines. Which is easy, surely? I mean the power of a big leisure business like Lambert's. Surely . . . (*He looks across the room.*) You'd stand by me. With all your sports shops and ice-rinks and hotels.

There is a pause.

Money isn't everything. Lambert, surely, come on.

There is a long silence. LE ROUX *makes one of his characteristic moves to a quiet part of the newsroom, where he speaks to himself, all eyes upon him.*

LE ROUX. I keep on trying to push the little people into holes. But they won't stay in. They wriggle, they keep popping out. They refuse to be happy in there. (*He turns.*) I admire my Editor. I give him my backing.

QUINCE. Lambert . . .

LE ROUX. How can I not admire an Editor who delivers me a scoop? Scoops are our life blood. And his wife I understand, who brought it to him. (*He smiles across the room.*)

ANDREW. Thank you . . .

REBECCA. My God . . .

ANDREW. How wonderful.

BILL. Great. (*He gives the thumbs up sign.*)

LE ROUX. This is what we do. We send back the document unread. And we publish the name of the person who gave it to us so they can go to gaol. My God, what an exclusive.

He goes over and seizes the document from BILL's *desk. The team is left open-mouthed.*

I always love capturing criminals. It does the circulation good. And it's always spectacular. Big headlines. (*To* REBECCA.) What is the name of your informant? I'll write it on the bottom here.

ANDREW. That's impossible.

LE ROUX. It's all right, there's a little space.

LAMBERT *begins to pace.*

QUINCE. Brilliant.

LE ROUX. Oh this is really exciting. 'Whitehall Traitor Unmasked'. What did you say her name was?

REBECCA. I didn't. (*She walks across to* LE ROUX.) Andrew, let's go.

LE ROUX *lets her take the document. He speaks quietly.*

LE ROUX. This raises something I've been meaning to say for some time. (*To* ANDREW:) I think you should leave. You're fired.

ANDREW. What?

LE ROUX. You're confused. You're a very confused person. You have a left-wing wife and a right-wing proprietor. The tensions in your life are irreconcilable.

ANDREW. But . . . I just won. I just won the Golden Finger. Two hours ago I was Editor of the Year.

LE ROUX. I hate prizes for journalism. Why single anyone out? I like a paper to be . . . (*He spreads his arms in a sweeping, smooth arc.*) . . . uniform. Nobody special. Nobody who has to be bribed with prizes.

ANDREW. But I've been an incredible success.

LE ROUX. But what have you done? What does it add up to? Ask Leander.

SCROOP. Bugger all.

LE ROUX. I provided the formula. (*He picks up a copy of the* Victory.) It worked in South Africa. Page one, a nice picture of the Prime Minister. Page two, something about actors. Page three, gossip, the veld, what you call the country-side, a rail crash if you're lucky. Four, high technology. Five, sex, sex crimes, court cases. Then it's editorials, then letters. All pleasingly like-minded, all from Kent. Then six pages of sport. Back page, a lot of weather and something nasty about the opposition. There you are. (*He closes the paper.*) The only bit I hate is all those foreign correspondents. They're totally out of your control. They bring you extraneous suffering, complexity. Even now I never look at their little half page. (*He looks across at* ANDREW.) And what do you do? What is your daily function? You write editorials. That's all. (*He opens the paper.*) Is this yours? 'In summary, genetic engineering is neither a good nor a bad thing, it depends wholly on the use to which it is put.' Oh yes, Andrew. (*He smiles.*) You say that very prettily. But I think other people could put it just as well. (LE ROUX *looks at* ANDREW *for a moment then he frowns at something he has seen in the paper.*) What is this, Doug? This story caught my eye on page six.

FANTOM *crosses to him.* LE ROUX *sits down to work.*

The other JOURNALISTS *have all returned to their desks.* ANDREW *and* REBECCA *are left standing.* BILL *is staring in amazement.*

LE ROUX. Where's our cartoonist?

FANTOM. In the pub.

LE ROUX. Get him up. (*He looks up as* FANTOM *lifts a telephone.*) Andrew, you haven't left yet. Please clear your stuff out. You are an embarrassment. Can't you see we are all trying to work?

ANDREW. I'm sorry. I won't go. My staff is behind me. They just said.

The CARTOONIST *has entered, breathless.*

CARTOONIST. Yes, sir. (*He pants.*) I'm your cartoonist.

LE ROUX. Welcome. You don't make me laugh.

CARTOONIST. No.

LE ROUX points at the cartoon.

LE ROUX. Who is this?

CARTOONIST. It's . . . That's the Prime Minister.

LE ROUX. I simply don't recognise her. Her eyes are too big. (*He begins to draw with little squiggles on the paper.*) And she should have a hat. Hats are funny.

CARTOONIST. Oh. Er . . .

But FANTOM *puts a finger to his lips to signal him to be quiet. Meanwhile* ANDREW *has leapt on to the desk for a grand address, arms wide.*

ANDREW. I appeal to you all! Fellow journalists . . .

LE ROUX. Please, don't waste your time. I've never noticed journalists have much sense of professional solidarity, have you, Leander?

SCROOP. None.

LE ROUX. Journalists are not noted for standing up for one another. It is not in their nature. (*He waves a hand airily.*) But by all means try, go on, why not give it a go? (*He turns back.*) Now look. This Scottish butter story . . .

ANDREW. Fellow journalists!

BILL. Listen to him!

Everyone at once bends over their work, ignoring him.

LE ROUX. Today I need a reaction from an MP.

QUINCE. I'll do it. I'll say anything. Scots butter? Am I for or against it?

EATON SYLVESTER, in evening dress, comes into the room fast. He is distraught.

SYLVESTER. Christ Jesus, Chief.

LE ROUX. Oh my God, I've forgotten, the Princess.

SYLVESTER. What a fuck-wit. I need help. She's just sitting there, like a shag on a rock. Grinning at me. She doesn't seem to understand anything I say.

LE ROUX. What have you done with her?

SYLVESTER. Hold on, she's coming.

LE ROUX gets up.

LE ROUX. Everyone. Smarten up.

JOURNALISTS desperately straightening ties, smoothing their hair.

SYLVESTER. I told her the joke about the two abo nudists.

BILL. I can't stand it! I'm going to resign!

A small fat woman in a tiara and dazzling silver evening dress has entered and finds herself directly opposite BILL SMILEY. She carries a champagne glass. Her dignity of bearing is a little wobbly. She speaks in a strange, strangled voice. Her name is PRINCESS JILL.

PRINCESS. Hello. Good evening. How are you? Carry on. Act normally.

BILL. It's my life! My life!

REBECCA. I am going to publish! I will take it elsewhere! *The Usurper* will print it! You will regret this.

ANDREW on top of the table. He turns as she goes out.

ANDREW. Rebecca.

LE ROUX. Ma'am, I would like you to meet my ex-Editor.

ANDREW looks down with horror.

Mr Andrew May. Princess Jill.

PRINCESS. Good evening. Carry on. Act normally.

LE ROUX. Mr May is about to address my fellow employees on the subject of journalistic solidarity.

She looks up expectantly.

ANDREW. Revenge. I will have my revenge.

There is a silence.

Scene Two

In the darkness the newsroom vanishes. The NEWSVENDORS *return.*

FIRST NEWSVENDOR. NUCLEAR POWER STORY: MINISTER DENIES IT!

SECOND. THAT FLASK: THE STORY IN FULL! EXCLUSIVE! ONLY IN THE 'DAILY USURPER'!

THIRD. SPECIAL BRANCH VISITS THE 'DAILY USURPER'! EDITOR SAYS 'I'LL NEVER GIVE IN'.

FIRST. EDITOR GIVES IN.

REPORTERS, PHOTOGRAPHERS *and a TV crew with lights rush after* QUINCE, *who stops at an advantageous position and turns, grandly. An instant news conference has assembled. With a little brush he quickly brushes his suit. He adjusts his hair, the lights for the TV crew flare and . . .*

QUINCE. On behalf of backbench opinion I have spoken to the Minister. Who at the moment for reasons of National Security is not available to speak to you. Although off the record I may say —

At once the television lights die.

If you ring this number . . . (*He distributes cards fast, like a card dealer.*) You will get your stories straightened. I mean amplified. (*He turns back to the TV crew.*) Lights on.

The lights come back on.

The Minister emphasises that the publication of a leaked memorandum in *The Daily Usurper* raises *no* issues relating to the nuclear industry. But does, however, raise important issues of loyalty in public service. To whom is the Civil Service accountable? London or Moscow? Thank you, ladies and gentlemen.

The lights go off, he gives a little skip.

OK how about champers at Sweaty Betty's?

REPORTERS. Thank you, thank you Mr Quince, thank you very much!

They clear from the stage as the NEWSVENDORS *cross again.*

FIRST NEWSVENDOR. USURPER EDITOR TAKES HONOURABLE COURSE!

SECOND. EDITOR FOUND HANGED!

THIRD. SEX-PLAN DIET! YOUR THIRTY-FIFTH DAY!

SECOND. LEAK TRIALS STARTS MONDAY!

FIRST. VICTORY NEW SALES RECORD! UP AND UP WE GO!

As the NEWSVENDORS *clear there is revealed the large workroom of the* LE ROUX's *two million pound bungalow in Weybridge. It is decorated entirely in the Japanese style. A bare, slatted wooden floor, tiny wooden stools approximately seven inches off the ground. Sliding paper screens for walls. There is a small pond in the floor with a Japanese bridge over it.*

At the centre of the room LAMBERT LE ROUX *is standing with a long wooden pole in his hands. He is dressed in a pale yellow robe with a red sash.* DONNA LE ROUX, *also in the warrior robe, is standing with her pole locked against his.*

There is silence.

Then suddenly LE ROUX *whirls his pole above his head with a mighty Japanese shriek. She holds her pole horizontally above her head and takes one step to the right. His pole crashes against hers. They freeze in that position.* EATON SYLVESTER *appears rather nervously at the back of the room. He is plainly taken aback. He is in a blue blazer, grey flannels.*

LE ROUX. Ah Eaton. Come in.

LE ROUX *and* DONNA *break from their position.*

SYLVESTER. This is nice, chief.

LE ROUX. Of course. Your first visit. We are learning Toyinka. The Japanese art of personal attack. Donna, give him a pole.

SYLVESTER *backs away.*

SYLVESTER. I'm not sure I'm dressed for it.

DONNA. Here.

SYLVESTER. Hello Donna.

She has handed him a pole, he takes it awkwardly.

LE ROUX. In classical Toyinka the art is to aim your blows at the kidneys. The kidney is in the centre of classical Toyinka. Traditionally it is then followed by a blow to the head.

SYLVESTER. Look, Boss, I . . .

LE ROUX. It is very straightforward. (LE ROUX *moves over and stands opposite him.*) When I bring this stick down on your head you jump to the right. Are you ready?

SYLVESTER. Mm no I . . .

LE ROUX *attacks, bringing his pole down.* SYLVESTER *jumps aside.*

DONNA. He's getting very good at it.

LE ROUX. It's true. (*He drops his stick and embraces a nervous* SYLVESTER.) It's a hobby. I have to do something in private.

SYLVESTER. I like paragliding. Dropping out of the sky, and giving someone a fright. (*He smiles.*) This place is great, Chief. And you've got a pool. (*He stands at the edge.*) Is this the only indoor pool in Weybridge?

LE ROUX. It was Donna's idea. It connects to our swimming pool outside. She liked the idea of swimming through, reaching for a glass of saki and drinking it here. And then swimming back.

DONNA (*defensively*). All right.

LE ROUX. But then I had to point out to her that if she could swim through, so could anyone. Now we have a little metal grill down there. You have to hold your nose, swim down, undo the padlock and then you're able to swim through.

DONNA. It's all so typical. Back home that sort of thing isn't necessary.

LE ROUX. No. You have an electric fence around the compound. With armed guards. That does it.

DONNA. It's all so small in this country. The houses are so close together. You can't ride a horse properly because there are houses in the way.

LE ROUX. That's what happens when you leave civilisation. It's a Third World country, dear. (*He turns, an easy confidence between them.*) Darling, Eaton would like some raw fish.

SYLVESTER. I'm not sure . . . I wonder . . . can we do our business?

DONNA. I'll go and work.

She takes off her robe and hangs it up. She wears silver leotards underneath.

LE ROUX. Donna is writing a thriller. She does it by the way of Zen.

DONNA. They all have sexual intercourse and shoot each other.

LE ROUX. One of my companies will publish it.

DONNA. Back in a mo'.

She smiles and goes. SYLVESTER *is left extremely uneasy.*

SYLVESTER. I'm sorry, I wouldn't have come if I'd known you were . . . relaxing.

LE ROUX. Well, you're here. So you'd better speak.

LE ROUX sits down on one of the small stools.

SYLVESTER. We must move quickly, it's Quince.

LE ROUX. I've seen him fronting for the Minister of Defence.

SYLVESTER. That's right. He's the blue-eyed flying pundit. Last week he was on all four channels simultaneously.

LE ROUX. He takes on too many jobs.

SYLVESTER. He voted himself on to the select committee to decide what engine to put into the new Viper Night Fighter. He also took a thumping great retainer from Harpers, the American aero engine people.

LE ROUX. A good firm. I respect their machines.

SYLVESTER. He promised he could deliver the contract.

LE ROUX. But the Germans got it.

SYLVESTER. Harpers are furious.

DONNA has returned with a wooden plate of fish with a toothpick which she hands to SYLVESTER.

DONNA. There you are. Sushi.

SYLVESTER. Oh thanks very much.

She goes. He stands looking at the wooden plate.

SYLVESTER. Harpers have tipped off the Fraud Squad that Quince is deeply on the fiddle. Dodgy currency transactions. Too many bank accounts. He needs one hundred thousand in a bank called Barclays — remember? You have it in South Africa — and I mean, tacky this is . . . Croydon branch . . . (*He takes out a single card.*) I have the account number. By Tuesday.

There is a pause.

LE ROUX. No.

SYLVESTER shifts uneasily, looking for some way of disposing of his fish.

SYLVESTER. Look I think . . .

LE ROUX. No.

SYLVESTER. I don't like him either. He's a pathetic little shit.

LE ROUX. He knows nothing. He's out of his class. And that dreadful column he writes in my paper. All about 'discipline', and the custard puddings when he was wearing short trousers.

SYLVESTER. Sure. But busted he's useless. If we put him back together he can go on doing us some good. Sort this one out, and he'll get in the Government.

LE ROUX. And?

SYLVESTER. Well I do think we need the Government.

LE ROUX. Oh yes?

SYLVESTER *looks at him uncertainly.*

SYLVESTER. Don't you think?

LE ROUX. Not as much as the Government needs us.

SYLVESTER (*smiles*). No, well obviously that's right, but I do think you should stick by your friends a bit, Lambert.

LE ROUX. Why?

SYLVESTER. Quince did get you the *Victory*, after all. I like this idea we're building a pyramid. Slowly. So we have a network. Of contacts.

LE ROUX. Contacts? (*He looks puzzled.*) I don't have any contacts, do you? No, ditch everyone. You don't need anyone. With me, there's nobody left. I once had fifteen hundred people who worked for me in South Africa. Where are they now?

SYLVESTER. Yeah. Turnover's good. Fresh blood. Of course.

LE ROUX. No, not a turnover. Everyone. All the time. Get rid of everyone.

SYLVESTER. Yes but . . .

LE ROUX. What?

SYLVESTER. I'm thinking . . .

LE ROUX. What?

SYLVESTER. Does that include me?

LE ROUX *does not reply. But after a silence, he speaks.*

LE ROUX. The great friendships are founded on mistrust. Watch lions. Distrust spices a relationship.

SYLVESTER. Boss, it's 'we'. 'We' bought Fleet Street. 'We' got the sales up. 'We' worked the formula.

LE ROUX. Be careful, Eaton. I don't like the word 'we'. When you use the word, it's the beginning of a slippery slope. The next word you use is 'collective'. Then it's time for you to go and live in Peking.

SYLVESTER *looks at him, worried.*

SYLVESTER. Look, Boss, I do worry. You're getting out of touch. In this room. This place. All those statues of griffins in the drive. You do have enemies.

LE ROUX. I can't say that any of them matter. Are you saying Fruit-Norton is a serious threat?

SYLVESTER (*smiles*). No, of course not.

LE ROUX. I saw Fruit-Norton. On my video machine. A programme that went out at eleven o'clock at night. On the communist channel.

SYLVESTER. Channel Four?

LE ROUX. No, BBC 1. He has written some book about me called *Expelled From Paradise*. I think he is actually clinically insane. I don't know why they don't have the manhood to shoot me. I always sit with my back to the window at the Irving Club. They could get me from the street. A .44 in the back of the neck. But what do they do? They publish books which are all remaindered in Foyles.

SYLVESTER. Fact is, Boss, you've sacked so many people there's a club. For the ex-employees. There's a tie. With little guillotines on it.

LE ROUX. Yes, I've heard. It's a compliment.

SYLVESTER. There's only one who won't wear it. That's Andrew May.

LE ROUX (*strangely*). Andrew May.

There is a pause.

I miss him. There are so many journalists, opinionated, in pubs, being rude about each other. Obese. Fat. Every time they sit down they have this big lump in front of them, this great swathe of fat falling over their trousers — and then thinking they are the equal of the people they write about. But Andrew was different. He had a talent — so few of them do. He could make a page look sensible. And I liked him, his boyishness. He was soft, like a peach.

SYLVESTER *shifts.*

SYLVESTER. Yeah I suppose if you . . . Yeah.

LE ROUX. But what does he do? Waste his days at the Press Council, complaining about me. It's beneath him. He'll never get me that way.

SYLVESTER. Yes, but I've got a whiff there's something going on.

LE ROUX. Whiff? What is this? Where have you got this 'whiff'? (*Violently, advancing on* SYLVESTER, *grabbing him by the throat.*) Are you still friends with these people? Do you meet them in pubs? Have you been in a pub with Elliot Fruit-Norton?

SYLVESTER *shakes himself free.*

SYLVESTER. No, of course not.

LE ROUX. Then what? What are you saying, Sylvester? Are you losing your nerve?

SYLVESTER. No, it's just . . . I've heard rumours of meetings. All over the country. The dispossessed getting together.

LE ROUX. 'Dispossessed', what do you mean? (*Prowling, like a big cat.*) They are the establishment! They think they have a right. They think they are England. They hate me because I am an outsider! No old boy and old chap. I've broken their toys and now there are tantrums. But none of them are manly, none of them have the courage to fight. (*With swift, violent, martial arts movements.*) Come out! Come out of the woodwork! Come out of your little holes! Fight me you bastards, fight me!

SYLVESTER. J'sus Boss, you've gone Japanese.

LE ROUX *goes to a small shrine, on a stand against the wall. It displays a blurred photograph of a Japanese soldier's face.*

LE ROUX. Do you know this man, have you heard of him? Ken Yakashito. He came out of the jungle thirty years late. He did not know the war was over. He tried to kill a newsreel team when he came out. Thirty years he was in there, fighting his war. I will fight.

SYLVESTER. Yes, but you have to know what you're fighting for.

LE ROUX. Ultimately. Yes. But you can have some fun on the way. For instance, that paper.

SYLVESTER. What paper?

LE ROUX. *The Daily Usurper.* Get it, get it for me.

SYLVESTER. All right, I'll nip out, where's your nearest er . . .

LE ROUX. No, I don't want to read it. I want to own it.

SYLVESTER. What for? There's no point. It's a liberal paper.

LE ROUX. Not after I've bought it.

SYLVESTER. They haven't even got an editor since that guy topped himself.

LE ROUX. An editor who commits suicide is totally unreliable. He should never have been appointed in the first place. I shall buy the *Usurper* and then . . . (*With a huge, karate chop gesture.*) . . . close it down.

SYLVESTER. Boss, there's a negative side to your nature just lately, your yang is totally flattening your ying.

LE ROUX. The minute the ground feels firm underneath you your body dulls. Grows flabby. Flabby, Eaton! That's got to stop.

DONNA *comes back.*

DONNA (*to* SYLVESTER). You haven't eaten your fish.

LE ROUX has turned and gone to a concealed cupboard and taken out a freshly laundered loin cloth and robe.

LE ROUX. No, he doesn't dare to. He doesn't trust me any more.

The two men stare at each other.

You rave about conspiracy. Well, you may join them if you choose. Or you may stay to fight. (*He throws the loin cloth and robe to* SYLVESTER.) Take your clothes off.

A pause. SYLVESTER *touches his tie and begins to pull it off. A fade.*

Scene Three

At the centre of the stage facing front stand MICHAEL QUINCE, ANDREW MAY, REBECCA FOLEY *and* BILL SMILEY. *They are all wrapped up against the cold. Behind them are mackintoshed* MEN, *some in caps, hands in pockets. The front group all have betting slips and programmes in their hands and are shouting and waving with excitement. Arc lights blaze down on the scene. The enthusiasm of the front group contrasts with the dourness of the group behind, the habitual punters. A commentary blares.*

COMMENTARY. It's Jack The Lad from Summer Song, then Red Hot Poker making ground on Summer Song. Then behind Red Hot Poker it's Golden Anniversary, Golden Anniversary, the Fiddler, Born And Bred. Now at the front it's still Jack The Lad, Jack The Lad, no, it's now overtaking it's Summer Song, in the last moment, it's Summer Song, Summer Song. Second Jack The Lad, third Red Hot Poker.

They all turn away in disgust except BILL SMILEY *who whoops with joy. The front group go off, with the celebrating* BILL SMILEY, *as —*

FIRST MAN. Fuck that.

SECOND MAN. Dear oh dear, call that a dog race?

THIRD MAN. What you doing next?

SECOND MAN. Reverse forecast. Walk Tall and Green Pastures.

THIRD MAN. Green Pastures? Fuck that.

FIRST MAN. You'd be safer putting you money on a tin of Pal.

SECOND MAN (*aside*). Green Pastures? I must be losing my mind.

> The PUNTERS *drift upstage toward a dimly lit, long, ill-stocked bar.*

> Over the public address system, loud, the 'Fanfare For The Common Man'. Four DOG HANDLERS, all women, lead four greyhounds across the stage. The dogs are fine replicas, on wheels. They go off. The PUNTERS have gone. The middle-class group reassembles.

REBECCA. Well done, Bill. How much?

BILL. One pound twenty.

REBECCA. Oh great.

BILL. For a fifty pee stake! There's a dog called Green Pastures in the next race.

> QUINCE, *dressed in a fine quality coat with a black velvet collar, is wandering about at the back.*

QUINCE. I don't understand. The lavatories are locked.

> ANDREW *is carrying a Harrods carrier plastic bag crammed with books. His pockets are full of newspapers. He is reading a hefty volume as he shambles about.*

REBECCA (*to* ANDREW). Why don't you put those bloody books down?

ANDREW. I was hoping to read between races.

BILL. Give it a break.

ANDREW. It's all very well. This stupid magazine is now giving me twenty-five books a week to review. (*He looks at the cover of the book he is reading.*) *Strategic Discourses* by Hyram Mountjoy Junior of the American Institute For The Study Of World Disorder.

REBECCA. Oh Andrew, you're wasting your time.

ANDREW. I know. I know!

REBECCA. You wouldn't need to do all that stuff if you accepted your redundancy terms.

ANDREW. I can't! It's a principle. I can't accept!

REBECCA. Take the money. Why not?

BILL. I've tried to tell him . . .

ANDREW. I can't. It's a matter of pride. He's got to pay me properly or not at all. A real golden handshake. Two hundred thousand pounds. To humiliate him.

REBECCA. Andrew. You're being sued by your Access Card.

ANDREW. Don't worry, I can hang on. It just drives me crazy, looking at these papers. (*He pulls a newspaper from his pocket.*) This story. It's so badly done.

BILL (*glances at it*). Well it's Herbert, it's got Herbert written all over it.

ANDREW *scribbles on the paper with a ballpoint pen.*

QUINCE (*looking around*). Why can't people do these places up? It's as if they liked squalor.

REBECCA. I was the journalist with the ultimate story, from the Ministry of Defence. My contact, he was weak, he was old, he voted Tory. He trusted me. And I go and see him every week in gaol.

They look at her uneasily.

ANDREW. I know but . . .

REBECCA. How can you make a distinction between any of the papers? I told him to trust the *Usurper*. This 'enlightened' newspaper. Weak. When the Flying Squad arrived, the board held out for a few weeks, till the fines started. Then they handed the documents over. (*She suddenly grabs a paper from* ANDREW.) Nothing can be said through these things. (*She holds it high above her head in anger.*) Half the time you think what does it matter? We don't have any papers in this country any more. Then you pick up a copy of anything, say *The Daily Snake,* and you suddenly think . . . 'I'm white hot with anger. Why are these people trampling all over my mind?' (*She turns.*) I walked away. I got out. I did the job and stopped. I stopped writing for papers. I stopped reading papers. It helps. Why can't you do the same?

ELLIOT FRUIT-NORTON *sweeps on to the stage. He is dressed for country hacking. He has a shooting stick, a trilby, a husky jacket and a fine and huge pair of binoculars hanging round his neck.*

FRUIT-NORTON. Ah good evening.

BILL (*to* ANDREW). He's here.

ANDREW. Oh hello, Elliot.

BILL. Hi.

QUINCE. Good evening, Elliot.

FRUIT-NORTON. Rebecca, my dear.

REBECCA. Hello, Elliot.

FRUIT-NORTON. I trust you are all enjoying the facilities. The dinner lounge has a very passable buffet du jour.

QUINCE. We missed it.

FRUIT-NORTON. No matter. It's not long before we close it down.

QUINCE. Oh really?

FRUIT-NORTON. This whole track has to go.

QUINCE. But it seems rather popular.

FRUIT-NORTON. My policy as Chairman of the National Greyhound Racetrack Inspection Board is to close down *all* uneconomic dog-tracks. There are far too many of them in all sorts of confusing provincial towns, some of them with very similar names. Full of talentless people from the fringe of the dog world, selling Trotskyite newspapers at the point of entry.

They all look at him, bemused.

I plan to concentrate all our resources on a few, really tightly run, lavish dog-tracks, near London. I have christened these 'centres for canine excellence'.

BILL. Well. You must be a really popular chap.

FRUIT-NORTON. Yes I am, it's true. I'm a huge success at it. A classical education always suits one to these jobs.

ANDREW. And to conspiracy.

FRUIT-NORTON. Yes. As you say. This place is ideal, don't you think, for our purposes? Amongst the working class no one will see us. They are perfect camouflage.

QUINCE. But for what?

FRUIT-NORTON. I have to tell you I am forming a consortium to bid for *The Daily Usurper*.

There is a pause.

BILL. The *Usurper!*

ANDREW. I don't believe it.

QUINCE. My God.

REBECCA. Oh no.

BILL. Buying the *Usurper?*

ANDREW. Are you sure it's for sale?

FRUIT-NORTON. There have been heavy losses.

REBECCA. Serve them right. May they rot.

FRUIT-NORTON. I see here at this dog-track, a team. The bud of an idea. Michael, star columnist. Bill, features. Andrew, with your expertise you'd take the senior position.

ANDREW. Editor!

FRUIT-NORTON. Deputy Editor. The day to day running. I shall determine grand strategy myself.

BILL. A paper, God, a paper again . . .

ANDREW. How will we get it?

FRUIT-NORTON. I have assembled certain senior statesmen, sound men all. Like us, disinherited. Men who have done good

service for their country, but now find themselves spurned by
Downing Street. By hazard also victims of hurtful editorials in
the *Victory*. A small guerrilla force of ex-Prime Ministers. If I
mention the name of Sir Achilles Pringle . . .

QUINCE. You're joking.

FRUIT-NORTON. Pringle has let it be known, via a gesture, that
he will lend his name, his gravitas, to a truly 'one nation'
paper.

REBECCA. What the fuck does that mean?

ANDREW. It means being back in work . . .

REBECCA. One nation? Look around you.

FRUIT-NORTON. Think. It means more than that. It means
more than that. It means at last a platform to express our
common aversion. To an individual whom — I — need — not —
name. Who has done us all harm. And whom we may now
harm greatly in return.

There is a pause.

ANDREW. Yes I see.

BILL. Yes.

ANDREW. I get it.

BILL. This is exciting.

ANDREW. Yes I do begin to see the possibilities of this.

QUINCE. This is actually very attractive.

REBECCA. Don't, Andrew.

ANDREW. Please.

REBECCA. Forget Le Roux.

BILL. I must say, come on, be fair, Rebecca. We'd have twenty-
four pages! We could fill them every day with stories about
what a shit he is!

FRUIT-NORTON. I can see the idea is beginning to catch fire.

REBECCA. Andrew . . .

ANDREW. Rebecca, this is a professional discussion.

REBECCA. Oh is it? I thought it was more to do with spite.

ANDREW. What do you mean?

REBECCA. Revenge, obsession.

ANDREW. Well for Godsake, what do you expect?

REBECCA. And is that a good reason for running a paper?

ANDREW. It isn't just that . . .

REBECCA. Oh really? Remember, three lies in one day. Will you forget about Le Roux?

ANDREW. Yes.

REBECCA. Will you?

ANDREW. Yes.

REBECCA. Will you?

A long pause.

ANDREW. Will you please stop telling me how to live my life!

QUINCE. How can we make sure our bid will be successful?

FRUIT-NORTON. We have someone who is willing to help. A visitor. Someone has come out to us.

QUINCE. Who?

BILL. Who is it? Who wants to join?

QUINCE. This may be dangerous.

FRUIT-NORTON. Not if we're careful. I am delivering a mole, deep in. He insists our deliberations be confidential. Andrew?

ANDREW. Yes.

BILL. Yes.

QUINCE. Yes.

They look at REBECCA. *She turns away.* FRUIT-NORTON *turns and makes tick-tack signals, slapping his chest twice and raising an arm. Then at the back* EATON SYLVESTER *appears. He is in a camel-hair coat. He smokes a cigar and carries a four-pack of beer.*

SYLVESTER. This is a good place. You could make something of it. All it needs is a little investment.

ANDREW. I can't believe it.

SYLVESTER *holds up a fistful of notes.*

SYLVESTER. I've made two hundred quid. The dogs are too easy, don't you find that? There's no fun in it. You just keep on winning.

He moves towards them. Instinctively they step back.

SYLVESTER (*to* QUINCE). Hello Michael.

QUINCE. Eaton. Haven't seen you for a while.

SYLVESTER. No. You all look so scared. (*He opens his coat to reveal its silk lining.*) Look, I left my gun in the dashboard.

BILL. Is he joking?

ANDREW. I don't want to talk to him.

FRUIT-NORTON. Wait.

There is a pause.

ANDREW. What does he want from us?

SYLVESTER. Lambert Le Roux has gone mad.

A silence.

ANDREW. Have you been sacked?

SYLVESTER. Not yet. We get on, as ever. It's just . . . His days are numbered, that's all. For medical reasons. He's developing serious mental problems, in his mind. He's not the full quid anymore.

QUINCE. I guessed it. I knew it was happening. I knew.

QUINCE is very excited.

SYLVESTER. I never worked with one who didn't go crazy. It's power. He's developed extraordinary physical aggressiveness. He hits people with poles. Literally. Including Donna. It can get pretty ugly. He sits watching Leni Reifenstal movies.

BILL. Oh no.

SYLVESTER. Oiled pectorals. All sort of rippling, you know what I mean? And a great deal of shouting. And he's there wriggling his bottom. He's got his hands in his lap.

FRUIT-NORTON. I think we understand.

QUINCE. God how disgusting.

FRUIT-NORTON. The habits of Sparta.

SYLVESTER. I want to get out. (*He hunkers down to put the beer on the floor. He takes one can, he pulls the ring, it fizzes.*) I'm part of a crumbling empire. I want to loot the ruins before anyone notices.

There is a pause.

ANDREW. OK.

SYLVESTER. Lambert Le Roux will bid for the *Usurper*. So I understand will you gentlemen. (*He takes an envelope out.*) This is Lambert's bid. I'm willing to let you know what it is.

He stands, holding the envelope out. Nobody moves.

REBECCA. Don't trust him.

QUINCE. If we know, we can outbid him.

REBECCA. Have nothing to do with it.

ANDREW. No, I'd like a look. Just to know. It doesn't commit us.

QUINCE *suddenly moves impatiently across and grabs the envelope.*

QUINCE. Oh bugger it. Come on let's get on with it. (*He opens the envelope.*) Thirteen million.

BILL. Gosh.

QUINCE. Can we do more than that?

FRUIT-NORTON. Pringle has a small family bank.

BILL. Oh I see! Now I understand . . . why we want him.

QUINCE. We have no reason to trust you. What's to say you're not deliberately misleading us?

SYLVESTER (*grins, broadly*). Test me. Ask me all the Le Roux questions.

ANDREW. Do you wake up shaking with fury?

SYLVESTER. I do.

ANDREW. When you're driving, do you find yourself making up things you wished you'd said to him?

SYLVESTER. Sure. All the time.

ANDREW. You don't secretly admire him? Think in a way he's got a point?

SYLVESTER. No.

ANDREW. That's a phase I went through. Has there been . . . ?

SYLVESTER. What?

ANDREW. Personal humiliation?

SYLVESTER. He's totally without morality.

ANDREW. You've spotted that.

SYLVESTER *nods.*

He's one of us.

QUINCE. I'm not sure. I'd like it to be real. I hate Le Roux like the rest of you. But let's be clear. We also want to get at the Government. Oh God, I so want to hurt them as well.

FRUIT-NORTON. Well, that will be possible . . .

QUINCE. After all I did for them. Now I've become an unperson. I can't even catch the Speaker's eye. Sir Denton Rudge no longer calls me in for a grilling on TV. I'll never appear again on 'Speak Or Shut Up'. I have to sit at home shouting at the television like ordinary people. In a way that's the worst. When I had a column on the *Victory* my views had plausibility. People listened, they had to, I was given the space. Without it I'm a loon, a flat-earther.

SYLVESTER. You can have that space back.

QUINCE. Oh God, if I could trust you.

SYLVESTER *grins happily.*

BILL (*to* SYLVESTER). I don't understand. What's in it for you?

SYLVESTER. Money. A great deal of money. I want to see sunsets in every country in the world.

There is a pause.

I will sell you the dirt on Lambert Le Roux.

A silence.

FRUIT-NORTON. Cheque book journalism. Well normally, of course, I disapprove, but in this particular case the national interest is involved . . .

ANDREW. What sort of stuff?

SYLVESTER. There's a first wife in Manila.

ANDREW. I didn't know that.

SYLVESTER. A house prisoner. Her story alone. His early days, in South Africa. Blood was spilt.

ANDREW. I knew it!

FRUIT-NORTON. I always suspected it. It was inevitable. A man of that type. A foreigner.

SYLVESTER. He didn't do anything himself. He hired other people. Youths with knives. We burnt down a couple of warehouses. Print my story and you'll put a bolt through his head.

QUINCE. How much?

FRUIT-NORTON. Please not now, not the vulgar details.

ANDREW. I can see it! The *Usurper*. It will be a beacon, shining out.

BILL. That's right.

QUINCE. Do you know . . . I think we've got him.

ANDREW. It will carry analysis of the bias in Le Roux's papers.

SYLVESTER. Alongside the dirt.

BILL. Great. I've dreamt of this. There is such a thing as a decent journalist, I've worked alongside dozens of them and they're just never given a chance.

FRUIT-NORTON. A worthy ambition. Reinstate moral values.

ANDREW. Yes, well I think . . . discuss contents later. First thing is . . . Damn it! Let's celebrate. We've all made mistakes. We've all trimmed. I have, I've worked for him. But now at last we can found a paper that's decent and honest and will be . . . the end of Lambert Le Roux!

SYLVESTER. I'll drink to that.

FRUIT-NORTON. Waitress! Champagne, four bottles on ice. I want to get squiffy.

There is no one behind the bar.

QUINCE. Oh God yes, let's get drunk.

FRUIT-NORTON. Waitress! Waitress!

REBECCA has moved away and is standing by herself at the side of the area. ANDREW moves over and stands behind her. The others are clustered around the bar.

REBECCA. I can't. I'm sorry. I hate him too. But if you spend your whole life fighting him, the sad thing is you become just like him.

ANDREW. Just like him? How can you say that? We stand for something. And we need institutions. We must have the means and the courage to buy the means. And that's what we're doing.

REBECCA stands still. There are tears in her eyes but ANDREW does not see.

FRUIT-NORTON. Champagne, damn you! Champagne!

Scene Four

The NEWSVENDORS come on.

FIRST NEWSVENDOR. SHOCK SALE GOES THROUGH! NEW OWNERS FOR *USURPER*!

SECOND. *USURPER* GOES STRAIGHT FOR RIVAL'S
THROAT!

THIRD. LAMBERT LE ROUX: AMAZING REVELATIONS.

FIRST. WORLD'S MOST FAMOUS PROPRIETOR: IS HE
DOWN AND OUT?

ANDREW *enters, pursued by* REPORTERS.

REPORTERS. Sir, sir, please sir. Please sir, just give us
something.

ANDREW (*turns*). I take no pleasure in the public discrediting of
a man towards whom I have no personal animosity. For that
reason, I am unwilling to embroider or comment on the
charges contained in our articles.

REPORTERS. Please, please give us something, Mr May.

ANDREW. We believe that while there is a threat of criminal
proceedings in South Africa, our duty at the *Usurper* is to
continue publishing these articles.

REPORTERS. More to come is there?

ANDREW. By his silence, he condemns himself. If he can answer,
then let him answer. If he does not answer, then draw your
own conclusions.

He walks away, the REPORTERS *pursuing.*

REPORTERS. Trying to stop his knighthood, Andy?

ANDREW. I don't think he'll be getting one of those, do you?

They have gone. The NEWSVENDORS *come forward again.*

FIRST NEWSVENDOR. LE ROUX SHARES PLUMMET.

THIRD. LE ROUX EMPIRE IN TROUBLE.

SECOND. WHERE IS LAMBERT?

FIRST. LAMBERT LE ROUX, THE GUILTY SILENCE: I
HAVE NOTHING TO SAY.

*The stage is cleared. Behind, the Yorkshire moors. Vast open
space. Light. Wind. Greenery.*

At the very back, coming over the horizon are a small group

*of men identically dressed in husky jackets. They are all
carrying guns and they have fine quality boots. They advance
towards the front of the stage, form into a group facing front
and raise their guns simultaneously.*

*They mime firing. Then they move a few spaces to one side.
Mime again. Then a few paces back. Mime again.*

*At their centre is LAMBERT LE ROUX. He is hatless. He
breaks from the group.*

LE ROUX. Gentlemen. I want to walk on my own.

ONE MAN. It's a long way back to the road.

LE ROUX. It's all right. I'll find my way.

*The men look nervously one to another then they head off
silently back. LE ROUX stands a moment, waiting. Then, a
great distance from him, appears ANDREW MAY. He has his
trousers tucked into lozenge patterned socks. He carries a back
pack. Across the immense distance he sees LAMBERT LE
ROUX. They stare at each other. ANDREW makes a move to
walk off.*

LE ROUX. Yes it's me. Synchronicity.

*ANDREW stops and has to walk to LE ROUX. He stops, still
keeping his distance.*

ANDREW. I've been expecting this.

LE ROUX. I heard that you were here for a walking weekend.
Alone. Where is Rebecca? Is she well?

ANDREW. The Yorkshire moors are so beautiful.

LE ROUX. Yes. I am out killing birds. Shall I get you a gun?

ANDREW *smiles.*

ANDREW. I knew you'd contact me. I've been waiting.

LE ROUX. Yes.

ANDREW. I knew you'd seek me out. To get me to stop
publishing. I knew you'd offer me money.

LE ROUX. Yes. How much do you want?

ANDREW (*shakes his head*). No. Not this time. You can't buy me. I'm not for sale. Nothing you can give me will ever make me stop publishing.

LE ROUX. I see. You seem very sure.

ANDREW. I don't want to talk to you.

LE ROUX. That is what people say. They all say that. 'I don't want to talk to him.' But they do. Why is that?

ANDREW. I have no idea.

A slight pause.

LE ROUX. Go, by all means. Go back and chuckle with your chums. Have a giggle.

ANDREW. It's not personal.

LE ROUX. Of course it's personal. Everything is personal. Look who your chums are. Elliot Fruit-Norton.

ANDREW. Well I can see you and he have had your disagreements. But putting those aside, you must admit he is a very distinguished editor.

LE ROUX. He's a fool. A joke. Mickey Mouse has a Fruit-Norton watch.

ANDREW. All the brilliant people you've just thrown away!

LE ROUX (*smiles*). Like Michael Quince?

ANDREW. He has a great gift, Michael. For writing anything. He has brilliant contacts.

LE ROUX. They are valueless. Quince is simply the urinal in which the British Establishment leaks.

ANDREW. You talk like that because you know you're beaten.

LE ROUX. Beaten?

ANDREW. You're reduced to calling us all names.

LE ROUX. Not you, Andrew.

ANDREW. God knows what you call me. What you called me that morning when you woke up and read in the *Usurper* that we'd found your first wife. Her story about the man you had killed.

LE ROUX *looks at him, puzzled.*

LE ROUX. I don't understand what you want.

ANDREW. What do you mean?

LE ROUX. What reaction are you after in printing that sort of stuff? Are people concerned? Are they running in the streets, screaming my name? And are they burning my papers?

ANDREW. They will. We're getting a lot of letters. A hundred and forty-five to three, on our side.

LE ROUX. Oh well then, I see which way things are going. Letters. Goodness me.

ANDREW. You are angry, you must be angry. We called you a murderer.

LE ROUX (*nods wisely*). Yes. To what end?

ANDREW. Well . . . For God's sake! To what *end*? Well, to shame you. Make you suffer.

LE ROUX. Suffer?

ANDREW. We want to be rid of you. Rid the whole country of you. This perpetual distortion of the truth. It has an effect. It's insidious. This contempt for balance. Facts! Because of you British people's minds are fogging . . . clogging . . . decaying . . . silting up . . . with falsehood.

LE ROUX. I must say I haven't suffered much so far. You want me to have a mental breakdown?

ANDREW (*shouts*). Well, if necessary, yes! Also, to inflame public opinion. You haven't heard this yet, but there are going to be questions in the House.

LE ROUX. My, my, I begin to feel mentally unwell already.

ANDREW. Don't patronise me! With your technique. This is it. This is trouble. This is war. This is Watergate. This is the beginning of the end.

LE ROUX (*turns away*). Delusions! Does nobody see? What on earth is all this stuff about the truth? Truth? Why, when everywhere you go people tell lies. In pubs. To each other.

To their husbands. To their wives. To the children. To the
dying — and thank God they do. No one tells the truth. Why
single out newspapers? 'Oh! A special standard!' Everyone
can tell lies except for newspapers. They're the universal
scapegoat for everybody else's evasions and inadequacies. (*He
shouts at the top of his voice.*) It is a totally unworkable
view of the world!

ANDREW. You always told me to fight. I am fighting. I've got
you on the ropes. You can shout and bluster all you like.
We've got stuff that will kill you stone dead in England, for
ever.

LE ROUX *looks at him.* ANDREW *is exultant.*

LE ROUX. You are all weak because you do not know what you
believe.

He glances off stage. At once IAN APE-WARDEN *appears. He
is in an immaculate Burberry coat and city suit, with a bowler
hat. He wears black leather gloves.*

(*To* APE-WARDEN.) This is your man.

APE-WARDEN *moves across to* ANDREW.

APE-WARDEN. By the power invested in me . . .

ANDREW *backs away at once.*

ANDREW. What's this? What's happening?

APE-WARDEN *gets out a large envelope and* ANDREW *points
at it.*

No!

LE ROUX. Yes!

APE-WARDEN. By the power invested in me . . .

ANDREW. I'm not taking it!

LE ROUX. You have to take it. It's for you.

ANDREW. No!

LE ROUX. Yes, I'm suing you.

ANDREW. You can't sue! The lawyers say you can't sue! The
facts are correct.

LE ROUX. Are they?

ANDREW. Yes. An impeccable source.

LE ROUX. You mean Eaton Sylvester?

ANDREW. I'm not saying.

LE ROUX. But that's who you mean.

APE-WARDEN *advances again.*

APE-WARDEN. By the power . . .

ANDREW. No! (ANDREW *has to run across to avoid the advancing lawyer.*) It's all over town. You've had a row with Sylvester.

LE ROUX. Have I?

ANDREW. You've fallen out. You fired him. You no longer speak.

LE ROUX. We're spending the weekend together.

ANDREW. That's not true. He's given us his story, we've paid him. I 'phoned your first wife in Manila.

LE ROUX. I don't have a first wife. Donna is my true love.

ANDREW. But this woman said . . .

LE ROUX. A secretary. I have extensive interests in the Philippines. She is a star of the local Dramatic Society. With a gift for tragedy — and lurid invention.

ANDREW (*shaking his head*). I took a deposition from a man in Pretoria! He claimed you'd shot him in the leg.

LE ROUX. I have many friends in Pretoria. Rugby players.

ANDREW. But it's a legal deposition! I have it in a safe, in the office.

LE ROUX. Examine it. It's signed Donald Eende. Eende is Afrikaans for duck.

He makes a duck's quacking noise.

APE-WARDEN. Inadmissable.

LE ROUX. We gulled you.

ANDREW. Gulled?

LE ROUX. You're dead. Eaton sold you a pup. He is the great salesman. You printed lies about me, and now you must pay.

APE-WARDEN *advances once more.*

ANDREW (*hysterically*). Get him off me! Please! Don't let him near me! Give me time, let me think . . .

LE ROUX (*to* APE-WARDEN). Do this elegantly. Put it in his pocket. Stuff it down his shirt. Stick it in his mouth. The writ for libel is such a little beauty. It goes right down their throats. They choke. You have such progressive judges in this country. I love it here.

APE-WARDEN *advances once more.*

ANDREW. Get him off!

LE ROUX. You think it is you who has the monopoly of feelings. But no, you hurt me, so I hurt you back.

ANDREW (*screams*). Get him off! Get him off! No, I won't take it.

LE ROUX. You have to. It's yours.

ANDREW. I won't! I can't! I can't stand it!

APE-WARDEN. He has to take it.

LE ROUX. He will.

ANDREW *stands with his hands above his head.*

LE ROUX. I am a man on a moral mission. I want people to see life as it is. I want them to see their real situation. (*He points to the writ.*) I thought at one time, I shall have to buy the *Usurper* in order to close it. Then I had a much less costly idea. You buy it. Then I sue you. And bankrupt you. And scatter my enemies.

LE ROUX *smiles.*

ANDREW. No!

LE ROUX. You know you understand now. Every nerve in you is screaming. Get down on your knees.

ANDREW. What?

LE ROUX. Beg.

There is a pause.

Haven't you got there? Don't you see it yet, Andrew?

ANDREW. What?

LE ROUX. Reality. You know you want to do it, in your heart, a deep longing. Do it now, Andrew.

There is a pause.

Ask me for a job. Down.

ANDREW. No.

LE ROUX. Yes.

ANDREW. No.

LE ROUX. Yes.

ANDREW. No.

LE ROUX. See things as they really are. To everyone I pose a question. I am the question.

ANDREW. And what is the answer?

LE ROUX. People like you.

APE-WARDEN *takes one step towards* ANDREW. *But before he reaches him he stops. He drops the envelope on the ground.*

APE-WARDEN (*quietly*). It's served. Although he doesn't touch it, that's the law.

There is a silence. Then impulsively ANDREW *reaches down and throws it back in* APE-WARDEN's *face.* APE-WARDEN *jumps into the air with joy.*

He touched it! He touched it!

LE ROUX. Control yourself, man. (LE ROUX *moves quietly and picks up the envelope.*) I come to this country to organise your lives. I do nothing. People fall before me as if they had been waiting. Why should I lift a gun? People disgrace themselves around me. 'Oh he's not as bad as I expected.'

From you alone there is a trace of resistance. But you seem to
have no idea how to use it, how to destroy. You should hit
a man in the face to make his face disappear. In my house I
have a thousand books. But I don't need to read them. My
mind is made up.

A pause. Then ANDREW *sinks to his knees.* LE ROUX *seems
momentarily lost in thought.*

I had a hotel in Bloemfontein. Just three hundred bedrooms
or so. And the hotel had a copying machine. On the à la carte
menu they did a little drawing, 'Chef of the day'. Then I found
a very witty waiter who wrote things about other hotels.
About less good hotels. It became fashionable in Bloemfontein
to eat in my hotel and read these little comments. Then I
thought 'Oh people will appreciate this more if they have to
pay for it'. And the menu turned into the *Bloemfontein
Gazette.* (*He smiles again.*) I'm still not interested in papers. I
like the *Victory*'s name. I'm thinking of concessions. *Victory*
tea-towels, *Victory* pillow cases, exploitation. I have many
new ideas late at night. I struggle with the great melancholy of
business. (*He shakes his head.*) Good papers are no good.
There's no point in them. All that writing. Why go to the
trouble producing good ones, when bad ones are so much
easier? And they sell better too.

ANDREW *looks up. He is still on his knees.* LE ROUX *nods
to* APE-WARDEN *to leave tactfully. He does so.*

ANDREW. I'm beaten, I know. The landscape is blasted. Every
decent hope people had, blasted. I just cling to this idea of
the language. That a sentence means something. Hang on to
the sentence. 'On the one hand, on the other . . .'

His voice dies. There are tears in his eyes. LE ROUX *walks
to stand behind him. He leans forward.*

LE ROUX. Editorial freedom. You never used it when you had
it. It is fast gone. Why should you deserve freedom any more?

He puts the writ gently in ANDREW's *mouth. The stage
darkens. A wind blows across the moor. Then* LE ROUX *walks
away, 'ti-tum ti-tumming' a tune to himself, as the moors are
overtaken by the incoming scene.*

Scene Five

At once the theme that LE ROUX *is humming is picked up by an unseen orchestra.* CHORUS GIRLS *and* BOYS *in spangled hats and suits dance on doing* The Daily Tide ZINGO *commercial.*

LE ROUX goes off as a scruffy, bewildered working MAN *is dragged into the limelight by two* GIRLS *in bikinis. They force him to the centre of the stage in a spotlight. He is blindfolded.*

HANNON SPOT enters. He is in a white suit with a yellow bow tie. He blares into a microphone. He has a broad cockney accent.

SPOT. Hello ladies and gentlemen, my name is Hannon Spot, and as Editor of the *Tide* I am proud to introduce our million pound winner!

From the side of the stage comes a huge twelve foot long cheque signed 'Lambert Le Roux'.

With the money he is hoping to start a small micro-chip business in a green field in a Government Redevelopment Area grade two. Right rip it off, Anthea. (*He kisses him.*) 'Ere you are, mate! Don't drink it all at once.

GIRLS *and* WINNER *exit.* SPOT *steps forward.*

And all you happy people out there, watching me now, remember! There is a tide in the affairs of men that can win you big, big, money. As we say in Fleet Street, the *Tide* comes in every day and splashes round your naughty bits. Byee!

Music, applause. They all go off. Behind, a new set is already established. The newsroom of the Tide. *White tiles. Green paint. Scruffy. An atmosphere of hectic activity in contrast to the antiseptic calm of the* Victory.

SPOT *skips on to the set and shouts at the top of his voice.*

Come on, you bastards! Keep working. Bert, over here.

BERT. 'Ere I come, Boss.

SPOT. This story about a talking horse. The horse that talks to itself. In Wiltshire.

BERT. It's a great story. Or is it rubbish, Boss?

SPOT. Be a better story if it was a pig.

NIGHT EDITOR. Forty minutes to edition time!

YOUNG JOURNALIST. Oh Jesus, oh God I can't cope.

Frantic activity.

BERT. What do you mean, Boss? Give me guidance on that one.

SPOT. I'm saying let's find a talking pig. Get a library picture of a pig and then sort of wiggle its mouth about.

BERT. Oh yeah we did that on *The Daily Snake*. Only then it was a goldfish.

YOUNG JOURNALIST. Please stop it, stop it, they're taking over my mind!

A COMPOSITOR *comes on.*

COMPOSITOR. Just asking. I mean, am I meant to be setting this up?

SPOT. Sure. What's wrong with it?

COMPOSITOR. This Editorial. 'To the Leader of Her Majesty's Opposition: jump in the khasi.' Is that it?

SPOT. What's the matter with it?

COMPOSITOR. Bit short in't it, for an Editorial? There's a paragraph missing?

SPOT. Print it in bloody great letters. Get a photo of an 'ead and a lavatory bowl. Then turn the 'ead . . . that way up. (*He turns his hands strangely.*)

COMPOSITOR. Oh, visual joke. Oh that's all right then. I thought it was just extraneous abuse.

ANDREW MAY *and* BILL SMILEY *enter from one side,* LAMBERT LE ROUX *and* EATON SYLVESTER *enter from the other.*

SPOT. Everyone! Stop workin'!

There is a sudden silence.

ANDREW. Lambert, how are you?

LE ROUX *holds him by the hand. He speaks to the newsroom.*

LE ROUX. There is more rejoicing in heaven over the one who returns to me than there is over the ten thousand lazy bastards who are loyal. (*He turns to* ANDREW.) Hannon, do you know Andrew May?

SPOT. Don't tell me. I've guessed it.

LE ROUX. Andrew is now in charge of the *Tide*.

SPOT. Oh, right.

LE ROUX (*shouts*). Everyone! We've got a new Editor. (*He points at* SPOT's *head*.) Not this one. (*He points at* ANDREW's *head*.) This one. (*Scattered applause*.)

SPOT. Congratulations, old cock.

The VOICE *cries again.*

VOICE. Thirty-five minutes to edition time!

Bells ring, numbers flash. LE ROUX *moves again. Activity heightens even further.*

LE ROUX. Let's get on with it.

SPOT. Right. Well. What was I doing one minute ago? When I was Editor. I'll show you the big tits competition. That's your first priority.

SPOT *and* ANDREW *leaning over a desk.*

SYLVESTER (*to* LE ROUX). This is his contract, Andrew May's terms of employment.

LE ROUX. I'll sign it now.

LE ROUX *goes through the contract crossing large chunks out.*

SPOT. We're looking for the biggest pair in England.

BILL. Andrew . . . It's an illusion, we can never work here.

ANDREW. Look Lambert's promised me we just have to do this for a while. Just for six months.

BILL. Then what?

ANDREW. Then he'll give us the *Victory*.

SPOT. We're on the look-out for silicon fraud.

He starts throwing out photographs of breasts.

LE ROUX (*a sudden cry*). Rights! Rights! All this nonsense about rights.

BILL. But Andrew . . .

ANDREW. What? Tell me, what's the alternative? Elliot Fruit-Norton? He's working with an old cyclostyle machine. He pays out-of-work actors to distribute his newsheet in Fleet Street pubs. He's a looney. I don't want to be a looney.

SPOT. At this job you get good at spotting a fraudulent tit.

LE ROUX. Signed. (*He waves the contract.*) Andrew?

ANDREW. Oh, fine. (*He turns on* BILL.) You're as bad as Rebecca. I don't want a best friend, I don't want a wife. I want this job!

A pause.

Why don't you fuck off?

BILL. Why don't you fuck off?

ANDREW *goes into an hysterical rage.*

ANDREW. Get me the picture editor! These tits are no good. These tits are terrible! These tits are terrible!

BILL, *backing away. Then he goes off.*

Oh God I feel better.

SPOT *is skipping across to* LE ROUX.

LE ROUX. Hannon.

SPOT. Here I come, ex-Boss.

LE ROUX. I'm making you Editor of the *Victory*.

ANDREW *looks across the room, the pictures in his hands.*

SPOT. Is that a good idea?

LE ROUX. I've appointed you.

SPOT. Oh well, I'll get on over there.

LE ROUX. No need.

Through the door are pouring twelve upper-class
JOURNALISTS *in suits carrying chairs on their heads, papers,*
typewriters.

I've decided to combine the two newsrooms. I'll cut both
papers in half. Up market, down market, it's all the same stuff.
And we do the same things to it.

SYLVESTER *strides amongst the mob of* JOURNALISTS
distributing notices of dismissal.

SYLVESTER. You're out, you're out, you're out . . .

LE ROUX *gives* SYLVESTER *one.*

LE ROUX. Eaton. You're out.

From the centre of the newsroom, causing silence and stillness,
ANDREW *shouts.*

ANDREW. Stop all this chatter! Get back to work! Work you
bastards, work!

LE ROUX. Gentlemen. We have a new foreman. Welcome to the
foundry of lies.

The bustle of the newsroom begins again, a crescendo of noise.

*Further titles in the
Methuen Modern Plays series
are listed overleaf.*